Million Dollar Careers

D1737512

WetFeet Insider Guide

Helping you make smarter career decisions.

WetFeet, Inc.

The Folger Building
101 Howard Street
Suite 300
San Francisco, CA 94105

Phone: (415) 284-7900 or 1-800-926-4JOB
Fax: (415) 284-7910
Website: www.WetFeet.com

Million Dollar Careers

ISBN: 1-58207-545-X

Table of Contents

Introduction

What's that you say? You'd like to be rich? Join the club. Wanting to be wealthy is not exactly a rare sentiment. If you make it, though—if you do manage to become wealthy— you'll be in fairly exclusive company. You'll be able to do things like join expensive country clubs, stay only in luxury lodgings when you travel, drive high-end cars, and live in a nice home (and maybe buy yourself a vacation home or two). And you'll be able to engage in some serious philanthropy, to boot.

The million-dollar question is, How does one get wealthy? Unless you're lucky enough to inherit millions of dollars, you're going to have to work to get rich. But what kinds of jobs are most likely to get you there?

Today is your lucky day, dear reader. We've done the work of identifying what some of the best careers are for those who want to get rich. This guide profiles 20 such careers, from accounting firm partner to film producer to rock star to venture capitalist.

There are a number of features common to many of these careers. In most cases, these are not careers that anyone can do. They require hard work, years of commitment, an extraordinary inner drive, and, in many cases, special talents that most folks just don't possess.

There's another feature that's common to careers that can make you rich. Take a look at the Forbes 400, *Forbes* magazine's annual list of the 400 richest Americans (a portion of the 2004 list follows this Introduction). Do you notice a commonality among the bulk of the people on the list? It's *equity*. Most of the people on the list *owned* the business that made them rich (or are descended from rich business owners). It's no coincidence that many of the careers profiled in this guide, from accounting firm partner and consulting principal to entrepreneur and real estate developer, involve an equity interest in a business; the appreciation of a business's value is where most of the wealth of the richest of the rich comes from. Even some of the careers that don't necessarily involve business ownership involve the ownership of a popular product. Film producers (and sometimes screenwriters) receive a percentage of their products' profits, for instance, as do pop, rock, and hip-hop stars.

Those careers in this guide that do not involve business or product ownership require extraordinary talent—in many cases, God-given talent. If you can't run or jump very well, for instance, there's very little chance you'll make it as a professional athlete. And if you don't look comfortable in front of the camera, it's exceedingly unlikely you'll succeed as a Hollywood actor. (With some rare but notable exceptions, of course. Does the name Arnold ring a bell?)

Each of the 20 career profiles that follow include a look at how well high achievers can do financially, a basic job description, the career paths typically taken by the most successful people in the field, and the formal requirements and personal attributes needed to succeed. We also provide an estimation of the odds of achieving great success in each career, with the odds of making it to the top in each career rated "poor" or "fair." (It's no accident that the odds are not "good" for getting wealthy via these careers. For most of these careers, it's either very difficult to break into, or it's very difficult to make it to the top of the compensation heap, or both.) In addition, each of these career profiles is accompanied by a list of additional resources, should you want to investigate a particular career further, and a short bio of a notable practitioner of that career.

We hope everyone who reads this book does indeed get rich. Failing that, we hope everyone who reads this book finds it helpful in embarking on a rewarding career. Good luck!

Before you dive in, we offer a little inspiration from those who have achieved the dream: Following are the 100 richest people in the United States, according to the 2004 Forbes 400 list. Note when more than one person occupies the same rank, it means there's a tie.

100 Richest Americans

Rank	Name	Age	Net Worth ($B)	Source of Wealth
1	Gates, William Henry III	48	48.0	Microsoft
2	Buffett, Warren Edward	74	41.0	Berkshire Hathaway
3	Allen, Paul Gardner	51	20.0	Microsoft, investments
4	Walton, Alice L.	55	18.0	Wal-Mart
4	Walton, Helen R.	85	18.0	Wal-Mart
4	Walton, Jim C.	56	18.0	Wal-Mart
4	Walton, John T.	58	18.0	Wal-Mart
4	Walton, S. Robson	60	18.0	Wal-Mart
9	Dell, Michael	39	14.2	Dell
10	Ellison, Lawrence Joseph	60	13.7	Oracle
11	Ballmer, Steven Anthony	48	12.6	Microsoft
12	Johnson, Abigail	42	12.0	Fidelity
13	Anthony, Barbara Cox	81	11.3	Cox Enterprises
13	Chambers, Anne Cox	84	11.3	Cox Enterprises
15	Kluge, John Werner	90	11.0	Metromedia
16	Omidyar, Pierre M.	37	10.4	Ebay
17	Mars, Forrest Edward Jr.	73	10.0	candy
17	Mars, Jacqueline	65	10.0	candy
17	Mars, John Franklyn	68	10.0	candy
20	Redstone, Sumner M.	81	8.1	Viacom
21	Icahn, Carl	68	7.6	leveraged buyouts
22	Knight, Philip H.	66	7.4	Nike
23	Ergen, Charles	51	7.3	EchoStar
24	Soros, George	74	7.2	hedge funds
25	Newhouse, Donald Edward	74	7.0	publishing
25	Newhouse, Samuel Irving Jr.	76	7.0	publishing
27	Murdoch, Keith Rupert	73	6.9	News Corp.
28	Broad, Eli	71	6.0	investments

Rank	Name	Age	Net Worth ($B)	Source of Wealth
28	Johnson, Edward Crosby III	74	6.0	Fidelity
30	Davis, Marvin H.	79	5.8	investments
30	Kerkorian, Kirk	87	5.8	investments, casinos
32	Arison, Micky	55	5.3	Carnival Cruises
33	Anschutz, Philip F.	64	5.2	investments
34	Bloomberg, Michael Rubens	62	5.0	Bloomberg
34	Warner, H. Ty	60	5.0	Beanie Babies
36	Abele, John E.	67	4.5	Boston Scientific
37	Geffen, David	61	4.4	entertainment
38	Bezos, Jeffrey P.	40	4.3	Amazon.com
38	Bren, Donald L.	72	4.3	real estate
40	Duncan, Dan L.	71	4.2	natural gas
40	Perelman, Ronald Owen	61	4.2	leveraged buyouts
40	Perot, Henry Ross and family	74	4.2	computer services
43	Brin, Sergey	31	4.0	Google
43	Kaiser, George B.	62	4.0	oil and gas, banking
43	Koch, Charles De Ganahl	67	4.0	oil, commodities
43	Koch, David Hamilton	63	4.0	oil, commodities
43	Page, Larry E.	31	4.0	Google
43	Wrigley, William Jr.	40	4.0	chewing gum
49	Moore, Gordon Earle	75	3.8	Intel
49	Nicholas, Peter M.	63	3.8	Boston Scientific
51	Menard, John R. Jr.	64	3.7	home improvement stores
51	Sorenson, James L.	83	3.7	medical devices, real estate
53	Crown, Lester and family	79	3.6	investments
54	Rowling, Robert	51	3.5	oil and gas, hotels, investments
55	Cook, William Alfred	73	3.2	medical devices
55	Goodnight, James	61	3.2	SAS Insritute
55	Lauder, Leonard Alan	71	3.2	cosmetics

100 Richest Americans (cont'd)

Rank	Name	Age	Net Worth ($B)	Source of Wealth
55	Taylor, Jack Crawford	82	3.2	Enterprise Rent-A-Car
59	Greenberg, Maurice Raymond	79	3.1	American International Group
60	Adelson, Sheldon	71	3.0	casinos, hotels
60	DeVos, Richard M.	78	3.0	Alticor
60	Kroenke, Ann Walton	54	3.0	Wal-Mart
60	Lucas, George	60	3.0	Star Wars
60	Tisch, Preston Robert	78	3.0	Loews
65	Bass, Robert Muse	56	2.9	oil, investments
65	Van Andel, Jay	80	2.9	Alticor
65	Wexner, Leslie Herbert	69	2.9	Limited Brands
68	Davidson, William Morse	81	2.8	glass
68	Hillman, Henry Lea	85	2.8	industrialist
68	Laurie, Nancy Walton	53	2.8	Wal-Mart
68	Schwab, Charles R.	67	2.8	discount stock brokerage
72	Lauren, Ralph	64	2.7	fashion
72	Perenchio, A. Jerrold	73	2.7	Univision
74	Filo, David	38	2.6	Yahoo
74	Jobs, Steven Paul	49	2.6	Apple Computer
74	Johnson, Barbara Piasecka	67	2.6	inheritance
74	Spielberg, Steven Allen	57	2.6	movies
74	Trump, Donald John	58	2.6	real estate
79	Bronfman, Edgar M. Sr.	75	2.5	liquor
79	Hughes, Bradley Wayne	71	2.5	Public Storage
79	Ingram, Martha R. and family	69	2.5	Ingram Industries
79	Johnson, Charles Bartlett	71	2.5	Franklin Resources
79	Rockefeller, David Sr.	89	2.5	Standard Oil, banker
79	Schulze, Richard M.	63	2.5	Best Buy

Rank	Name	Age	Net Worth ($B)	Source of Wealth
79	Simons, James H.	66	2.5	hedge funds
79	Stern, Leonard Norman	66	2.5	real estate
87	Bechtel, Riley P.	52	2.4	engineering, construction
87	Bechtel, Stephen Davison Jr.	79	2.4	engineering, construction
87	Blavatnik, Leonard	46	2.4	oil, coal, real estate
87	Udvar-Hazy, Steven	58	2.4	International Lease Finance
87	Zell, Samuel	63	2.4	real estate
92	Burkle, Ronald	51	2.3	supermarkets, investments
92	Hunt, Ray Lee	61	2.3	inheritance, oil, real estate
92	Huntsman, Jon Meade	67	2.3	chemicals
92	Pohlad, Carl	89	2.3	banking
92	Simplot, John Richard and family	95	2.3	potatoes, microchips
97	Butt, Charles C.	66	2.2	supermarkets
97	Helmsley, Leona Mindy Rosenthal	84	2.2	real estate
97	Saban, Haim	59	2.2	television
97	Spangler, Clemmie Dixon Jr.	72	2.2	investments
97	Yang, Jerry	35	2.2	Yahoo

Source: Forbes 400, *Forbes*, 9/24/04.

The Careers

Accounting Firm Partner

Actor

Asset/Portfolio Manager

Chief Executive Officer

Chief Financial Officer

Consulting Firm Principal

Entrepreneur

Fashion Designer

Film/TV Producer

Investment Banker

Investment Bank Sales and Trading

Law Firm Partner

Literary, Sports, or Talent Agent

Professional Athlete

Real Estate Developer or Investor

Rock, Hip-Hop, or Pop Star

Sell-Side Research Analyst

Surgeon

TV or Film Writer

Venture Capital Firm Partner

Accounting Firm Partner

WHAT YOU CAN MAKE

Surprised by the inclusion of this job in a book called *Million Dollar Careers*? You shouldn't be. Think about it: When we talk about the Big Four public accounting firms (Deloitte & Touche, Ernst & Young, KPMG, and PricewaterhouseCoopers), we're talking about firms that make billions of dollars of profit in most years. These are partnerships, which means a limited number of people—the partners—ultimately get to divvy up all that cash.

Big Four partners typically start at around $200,000 per year; depending on their particular responsibilities, the amount of business they bring in, and the performance of their firm, some partners can make a million dollars per year. National practice directors at Big Four firms reportedly earn in the seven figures.

JOB DESCRIPTION

By this point in your accounting career, you're pretty much done with the in-the-trenches accounting work. If you're an audit partner, you leave the actual poring over the clients' books to younger auditors. If you're a tax partner, you leave the actual digging through the clients' receipts and preparing tax returns to younger tax accountants.

Your job now is most likely more focused on three things. First, you're responsible for new-business development—for finding opportunities to make more money for your firm. Typically, this involves looking for ways you could help existing and new clients and then selling them on your ability to help them. Second, at this stage in your career, you're probably quite involved in developing the talent beneath you—in passing on your knowledge, and making sure that top talent continues to grow professionally and doesn't suddenly leave your firm. Finally, you review and sign off on the work being done by the people you manage—tax returns, in the case of tax partners, and audits, in the case of audit partners.

The sales part of the job description is especially important. If you want to make partner, says an insider, "You're expected to bring in clients, so you have to go to meetings and events and really be out there in the business world generating business."

MAKING IT

Typical Career Paths

Generally, your first few years in public accounting are considered a kind of training period focused on your professional development, so that you can transition from a generalist/team-player role to a more specialized position with management responsibility—especially if, like most starting accountants, you go to a Big Four firm or one of the firms at the top of the second tier of accountancies.

The career path is fairly set in stone for Big Four employees. They enter their firms as staff accountants (or, in some firms, as assistant staff). After 2 or 3 years, they move to the senior accountant level. Two or 3 more years lead to the managing accountant level. With 8 or 10 years of experience, they become senior managers. Finally, after 10 to 14 years, they make partner.

Almost no one is skipped over for these regular promotions; if they are, a pink slip is usually on the way. Insiders report that there is usually a wave of staff that leaves the Big Four after a couple of years, when they have qualified for their CPAs, and then another wave that leaves after they get a year of management under their belt. If you perform extremely well, you can obtain an early promotion.

In the Big Four, after your first couple of years or so on the audit side, you'll be required to specialize in a specific industry.

What It Takes

The vast majority of accounting jobs require at least a bachelor's degree from a 4-year university. In fact, according to the American Institute of Certified Public Accountants (AICPA), within the next few years, 48 states will require 150 hours of university education—30 hours more than for a regular 4-year degree—before you can even take the test to become a CPA. Currently, 45 states have adopted the 150-hour requirement, while the remaining states/jurisdictions continue to work toward adoption.

> **You're expected to bring in clients, so you have to go to meetings and events and really be out there in the business world generating business.**

While college is almost always a requirement, what you can study is beginning to broaden tremendously. With the rise of accounting software that's now taking care of much book balancing, accounting firms are looking to business and finance majors to work in accounting departments. Degrees in finance, business, and even management of information systems (MIS) are definitely good things to have in landing a job as a management accountant or internal auditor.

And once that bachelor's degree is out of the way, most accountants who go on to get a master's degree don't get a master's of accounting (MA). Much more popular are MBAs with a specialization in either finance or accounting. And again, any education you pick up relating to technology and information systems is going to be a big ace to carry around in your pocket.

Once you have school out of the way, the next step for many accountants is getting licensed. To become a CPA, even after 150 hours of undergraduate courses, in many states you need to work for about a year before you can take the exam.

Beyond the formal requirements, finance and accounting jobs require critical, detail-oriented thinking. If you have a knack for using numbers to understand patterns that influence business, you're going to be valuable to a company. If you can't crunch and analyze them, this isn't going to be the right job for you. You should also like, and be good at, solving problems and be able to think critically about the numbers you're working with.

While accountants need to be good at math and have strong analytical-thinking and research skills, attention to detail is usually considered more important. And to develop business relationships and close new business, accounting professionals find it necessary to develop strong written and verbal communication skills.

The AICPA strongly recommends that all accountants balance their technical business training with a classically liberal education. Furthermore, as business is increasingly being performed electronically, accountants need to pick up as much knowledge about computers and information systems as possible, not only to understand their utility but also to assess their value to clients.

 **INSIDER TIP**

Internal politics play a big role when it comes to staffing at the Big Four.

Why? Everyone wants to get put on good, visible projects that can help them advance up the career ladder. An insider says, "Your success depends on what kinds of clients you get put on. If you get put on clients that are a total mess, it changes the whole ballgame; you're working lots of overtime and are under a lot of pressure. Conversely, if you're put on a good project and the partner likes you, you have a chance to show your stuff. All this depends on whom you rub elbows with."

Finally, to make it to partner, you've got to be able to sell. Partnerships are handed out way more readily to "rainmakers"—those who can bring significant new business into the firm—than to wallflowers. So, if making partner in a big accounting firm is your career goal, as you move up the ladder, make sure you spend time networking with clients and prospective clients. Also, be sure to focus some energy on learning how successful partners win new business. Finally, since new partners are selected by the existing partnership, make sure to cultivate good relationships with the partners you come into contact with on your way up. This means saying yes to highly visible assignments, working long and hard when necessary, and accepting those invitations to golf outings and dinner parties more often than not.

While Big Four accounting firms recruit a very diverse crowd for their entry-level positions, at least in terms of race and gender, at the end of the long, hard slog to the partner level, it's usually white males who are still in the race. If being a partner in a Big Four firm is your career goal, *caveat emptor.*

The Odds: Poor

As a quick look at the numbers of new employees hired by the Big Four each year versus the numbers of new Big Four partners named each year will tell you, the odds of making partner are long. Partnership positions only go to those who've put in the hours and built the relationships necessary to stand out from their peers.

Each year, seeing the writing on the wall vis-à-vis their potential of making partner, many Big Four accountants take their hard-won experience and move to greener pastures. The good thing is that there are usually plenty of opportunities for people who move out of accounting; these jobs are great stepping-stones. Insiders say their exposure to a wide range of companies and industries and the vast responsibility given to them allows them to develop impressive skill sets, whether they want to hang out their own accounting shingle, go into finance in industry, or go into another profession entirely. One insider says, "When I look back on my 4 years in the Big Four, what I've learned is unbelievable. In college, it would have taken me 10 years to learn this much."

ADDITIONAL RESOURCES

American Institute of Certified Public Accountants (www.aicpa.org)

Beta Alpha Psi, an accounting and business fraternal organization (www.bap.org)

Careers in Accounting (WetFeet Insider Guide, available from www.WetFeet.com)

CPAnet (www.cpanet.com)

National Association of Black Accountants (www.nabainc.org)

Uniform CPA Examination website (www.cpa-exam.org)

PROFILE

R. Wayne Jackson, Accounting Firm Partner

If R. Wayne Jackson isn't as famous as some of the other people profiled in *Million Dollar Careers*, blame it on his job. Accountants typically work behind the scenes. In fact, if an accountant makes the newspapers, at least in recent years, usually it's because he's done something wrong—so most accountants don't mind staying out of the public eye, thank you very much.

Jackson is notable not for doing something wrong, but because in June 2004 he was promoted to the position of global leader of the Entertainment and Media Practice at PricewaterhouseCoopers (PwC), one of the Big Four accounting firms. Jackson originally joined PwC in 1979, after graduating from the University of Alabama. He was elected partner at the firm in 1991. In a career spanning more than 25 years, Jackson has worked on PwC's behalf for clients such as Time Warner, BellSouth, Turner Broadcasting System, New Line Cinema and Castle Rock Entertainment, and MCA/Universal. He left PwC briefly starting in 2000, to work for Concert, a joint venture between AT&T and British Telecom, but returned to PwC in 2003. He's recognized throughout the accounting industry, is a frequent speaker at industry events, and is known as an authority on issues such as corporate governance and financial reporting.

As global leader of PwC's Entertainment and Media Practice, Jackson oversees the firm's assurance, tax, and advisory work for companies in those industries. He is the firm's primary public spokesperson on issues relating to those industries, the head of the editorial board for the firm's annual international market forecast for the entertainment and media sectors, and the firm's main man when it comes to new business development with media and entertainment companies.

Actor

WHAT YOU CAN MAKE

Those few actors who make it to the pinnacle of their profession command immense compensation packages. Jim Carrey, for instance, was paid $25 million for his work in *Bruce Almighty*. Julia Roberts was paid $20 million for her role in *The Mexican*. Keanu Reeves made $15 million each for *The Matrix Reloaded* and *The Matrix Revolutions*. And Angelina Jolie received $7.5 million for her role in *Lara Croft: Tomb Raider*. And, famously, the cast members of *Friends* were paid nearly $1 million per episode toward the end of that show's run.

JOB DESCRIPTION

Basically, the job of an actor is to memorize his or her lines in a play, screenplay, or teleplay; rehearse as necessary with other actors and the director; and then perform his or her part in a compelling, believable manner in front of a live audience or rolling camera. But the specific job description of an actor depends on the role and the project. Some roles require an actor with special skills, such as the ability to dance or sing. Some roles require an actor to assume a foreign or regional accent. Some action-film or -program actors do their own stunts.

Aside from those who strike it big and become in-demand stars, actors must audition as if auditioning is a full-time job, sometimes going for years without a role. They must be prepared to accept rejection and criticism. A talented actor may not be cast in a given role because of his or her physical attributes: too short, too tall, wrong race, male, or female, or just plain not right.

Those who do well in the performing arts are creative, expressive individuals who are passionate about their craft. Patience, perseverance, and stamina—in addition to talent, practice, and a thick skin—are crucial to success. Actors may perform the same roles for months, sometimes years. Film actors must sometimes shoot the same scene over and over again. And regardless of how an actor is feeling—whether he or she is exhausted or in a bad mood—the show must go on.

One of the big differences between acting for television and acting for film can be scheduling. Regular actors on TV series basically have a regular job and are required to show up on the set on a regular basis during the show's production season. Film actors, on the other hand, often have more irregular schedules, putting in lots of hours while the films they're working on are in production, but having tons of time on their hands between projects.

In addition, film actors often have to do much more traveling than do their small-screen counterparts. TV productions may include exterior and location shooting, but those exteriors and locations will typically be near the studio where the bulk of shooting occurs. Films, on the other hand, can be shot entirely on location—which can mean spending months at a time far from home.

Finally, at the big-money level, actors usually have to spend a significant amount of time promoting themselves and the projects they're working on. A TV actor may have to make appearances on morning news shows during sweeps month, for instance, and a film actor may have to travel to Europe to do interviews just before her film is released overseas.

MAKING IT

Typical Career Paths

Whether your dream is screen acting (for films or television) or stage acting, in Hollywood or on Broadway, there are a variety of career paths actors can take. Some end up in regional theater troupes, some find lucrative careers in radio doing voice-overs, and others appear on daytime soaps or television commercials. (By some accounts, television commercials account for 60 percent of all acting jobs.) Sometimes, working actors (such as Mel Gibson or Jodie Foster) end up directing or producing their own films.

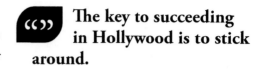

The key to succeeding in Hollywood is to stick around.

Most actors start performing in school or begin work as part of a technical crew and go on to get training in summer-stock theater companies or local stage productions. Initially, relatively inexperienced actors may work as extras in film roles, with few or no lines to memorize, or as understudies for off-Broadway shows. From there, with some luck, once they have developed experience, confidence, and credits, they move up to more challenging and larger roles.

What It Takes

In terms of formal requirements, union membership can be required for key jobs. For instance, any plum TV or film role will require the actor who plays that role to be a SAG (Screen Actors Guild) member. Beyond that, any successful actor will have a good agent with extensive industry contacts trying to get bigger and better roles for him or her.

Regardless of what you may think in your snarkier moments, the majority of successful actors have at least a modicum of talent—of the ability to play a role believably. At the million-dollar-career level, most also have at least a modicum of physical attractiveness. Successful actors are also hardworking (since acting often involves 16-hour days that start at 5:00 a.m.) and persistent (think of all those auditions . . .). Actors need a good understanding of human nature to understand and be effective in the roles they play. And they have to be flexible and resilient, since their careers will invariably include professional roadblocks, and since it's the rare TV, film, or stage project that does not include an occasional production snafu. Perseverance also plays a role in your success. As Marlon Brando put it, "The key to succeeding in Hollywood is to stick around."

Your audiences play a role, too: They are, in the end, the people you're working to please.

The Odds: Poor

There are maybe 75,000 working actors nationwide. Of those, only a few thousand make enough money to consider acting their full-time career. Of those few thousand, only a relative handful achieve the kind of success that we're considering here. Some of those actors work on Broadway; most are regulars on TV series or actors who regularly have significant speaking roles in films.

Still, every year, thousands of aspiring actors move to L.A. and New York in pursuit of their dream career. As Edward Norton once put it, "Anyone pursuing an artistic career is gambling, particularly if they know there are other things they can be doing. On the other hand, every year you're doing something you're not in love with is an equally damaging waste of time."

Anyone pursuing an artistic career is gambling, particularly if they know there are other things they can be doing.

Unfortunately for those who try acting as a career, if they don't make it, their acting skills don't transfer directly to other, more stable professional pursuits. The only other thing many actors are qualified to do is teach acting. However, many of the skills honed by actors can help them in other careers; for instance, acting ability can come in handy in careers such as sales.

ADDITIONAL RESOURCES

Actingbiz. Online Actors Resource (www.actingbiz.com) The Actor's Checklist (www.actorschecklist.com)

American Federation of Television and Radio Artists (www.aftra.org)

Screen Actors Guild (www.sag.org)

PROFILE

Katie Holmes, Actress

These days, Katie Holmes is probably best known for having the power to make Tom Cruise jump up and down like a chimpanzee on *Oprah*. But even before she became the love of Cruise's life, she was making quite a name for herself in Hollywood. She's probably best-known for playing Joey Potter in the old WB teen-angst drama *Dawson's Creek*, but in recent years she's displayed her acting range and garnered some solid reviews for her performances in films like *The Gift*, *Abandon* (for which she was paid $1 million), and *Pieces of April*.

Holmes was born in 1978 in Ohio. While she was in high school, her mother took her to L.A. to audition for TV roles. As a result of that trip, she was cast in the 1997 Ang Lee movie *The Ice Storm*. Next up was playing Joey on *Dawson's Creek*, which ran from 1998 and 2003. (She auditioned for the role via video, because she didn't want to miss playing her role in her high school production of *Damn Yankees*, which was being put on the same night as the *Dawson's Creek* auditions.)

Holmes's most recent role is the lead sexy-babe in the next movie in the Batman series, *Batman Begins*. Oh, yeah—and, most likely, getting involved in Scientology, as most of Tom Cruise's real-life love interests seem to end up doing.

 ON HER MILLION DOLLAR ACTING CAREER

"I love acting and I suppose taking risks is a huge part of being an actress. That's thrilling to me—taking those risks. It's almost addictive. I suppose I'm one that enjoys a good ride, a good journey."

Asset/Portfolio Manager

WHAT YOU CAN MAKE

Average annual salaries for portfolio managers range from $200,000 to more than $1 million. The top fund managers of the biggest funds earn basis points on the management fee the fund charges investors, so the more money they manage, the more money they make. Managers of high-performing funds can make $10 million to $15 million a year.

JOB DESCRIPTION

Asset managers, also called *investment managers* or *money managers*, are responsible for investing the assets of a group, institution, or individual according to specified management goals. Asset management companies are typically organized around funds and run by portfolio managers. These people have a coterie of analysts to support them.

As a portfolio manager you're at the pinnacle of the asset management world. At some level, the job is pretty straightforward: Your company, be it a mutual fund, pension fund, or other fund, has specific investment goals, and your job is to pick a portfolio of stocks, bonds, or combination of the two, to make the highest returns for investors given those goals. The job is analytical, strategic, and on some level, sales oriented.

All of the following might be part of a day in the life of a portfolio manager: You order traders to execute the purchase or sale of securities. You meet with the CEO of a company you're thinking of investing in to grill him about the business. You huddle with your assistant manager or analysts to go over stock picks, optimization of short-term instruments like money market securities, and your fund's alpha rating. You then work with them to tweak the financial model that's the basis of your day-to-day fund management. You spend some time getting briefed on industry developments and corporate intelligence. Add to that client-relations work. If you are managing a pension or other asset fund, you might brief a charitable foundation on your investing strategy for a sales call or meet with the investment manager of a current client to review your fund's performance.

The asset management industry breaks down into five major categories.

WHAT INSIDERS SAY

"My job is like a window on the world. To be good, you have to keep up with a constantly changing world. And the stock market is like a daily jolt of adrenaline, whether it goes up or down."

Mutual Fund Management

Mutual fund management includes funds raised with money from individual shareholders and institutions that invest in any combination of stocks, bonds, and money market instruments, according to very specific investment goals, and adhere to strict governance laws. Mutual funds are regulated under the Investment Company Act of 1940. True mutual funds are considered "open-ended"; that is, investors can buy or sell shares at any time based on the value of the assets at that time. Closely related to mutual funds are closed-end funds, which offer a fixed number of shares; exchange-traded funds, which trade on major exchanges; and unit investment trusts, which offer dividends or interest to their shareholders and have set termination dates.

Retail Asset Management

Retail asset management includes a host of services, primarily for high-net-worth individuals, that includes trusts and professionally managed accounts (in which investors consent to leave the investment decisions to the professionals, much to the delight of trustafarians everywhere who can better spend their time on independent film projects or following Green Day concerts). A client's net worth or level of investable assets usually determines the level of service he or she receives, from call center to personal banker. Those firms that cater to high-net-worth clients tend to offer more exotic investments, such as private equity funds, in part because they're not restricted by regulations designed to protect smaller nest eggs from risky investments. Unlike commission-based brokerage accounts, retail asset managers usually charge a fee based on a percentage of assets under management. Major brokerage houses, such as Merrill Lynch and Morgan Stanley, and many specialized asset management companies offer retail asset management services.

Hedge Fund Management

Once thought to be arcane, volatile, and the province of Nobel Prize winners such as Myron Scholes, hedge funds have suddenly become arcane, volatile, and wildly popular. Drawn by the potential to make millions, if not tens of millions, each year, MBAs are pounding on the doors of these firms.

Their track record in down markets—hedge funds consistently beat mutual funds when indexes fall—has piqued the interest of smaller investors, even as their records start to look slightly less stellar. The firms, in turn, have noticed. Some hedge funds accept investments as little as $25,000 from individual investors. Asset managers have launched funds of hedge funds—vehicles that use some of the same investing techniques as a traditional hedge fund, such as short-selling, but mitigate the risk by spreading the investment across several hedge funds. Institutional investors such as pension funds and foundations still account for a big part of hedge fund contributions. Regardless of who's investing, their numbers have grown so much that they now equal the number of mutual funds. Compared to about 100 in the early '90s, investors can now choose from about 8,000 hedge funds.

Institutional Asset Management

Institutional asset managers invest money on behalf of corporations, insurance companies, pension funds, endowments, and charitable foundations. Asset managers offer this wide range of clientele a picnic basket full of investment goodies, including money market funds, equity investments, fixed-income products, 401(k) administration, and active and indexed funds.

Pension and Retirement Fund Management

Pension and retirement fund management is exactly as the name implies. Back in the good old days when workers didn't have to fund their own retirement plans through 401(k)s and IRAs, employers used to set money aside for their employees' retirement. Ah, how times have changed. Nevertheless, pension funds do exist; the largest of these, the California Public Employees' Retirement System (a.k.a. CalPERS), has $185 billion in assets. As you might guess, the most populous states in the union have the largest employee retirement funds; following CalPERS are the California State Teachers' Retirement System ($126 billion) and the New York State Common Retirement Fund ($119 billion). The largest private pension plan is that of General Motors, with $91 billion in assets. Pension plans either invest assets themselves or rely on an institutional advisor to invest for them.

MAKING IT

Typical Career Paths

The previous rung on the career ladder for most portfolio managers is investment or research analyst, or possibly junior portfolio manager.

Insiders recommend doing an investment banking analyst program to get some Wall Street cred (read, analytical skills and industry knowledge) before trying to break into portfolio management.

Undergraduates with their hearts set on a career in asset management should take as many statistics and accounting classes as possible to prove that they can handle all of the number crunching and financial modeling that the profession requires. Undergraduates may be able to land jobs as research analysts, though competition is tough and they may be going up against candidates with MBAs.

If you're really serious about the profession, start with a job in sales, marketing, operations, or trading at an asset management firm, then consider going back for an MBA or taking your CFA before switching into asset management per se. You may also consider a 2-year analyst or research position in investment banking. Such jobs are more plentiful and provide excellent training for asset management.

 INSIDER TIP

"An MBA is the most useful route to becoming a fund manager. People should also be willing to take a job beneath their talents when they start out. If you show good judgment, you can advance rapidly, so be willing to take whatever offer comes your way. You've also got to be willing to relocate to a big city."

Generally, MBAs come aboard as researchers or analysts. Analysts and researchers generally serve at least 2 years before they come up for consideration as fund managers. It's important to note, however, that not all asset management firms see the MBA as a key to success. The degree "is not that important for portfolio management," says one insider. "If you want to become a manager and run a marketing program, then perhaps it's useful. The CFA is the designation given the most reverence in asset management."

You are more likely to get an asset manager position earlier if you run smaller portfolios for institutional asset managers or private banks that offer services to the wealthy. On the mutual fund side, you might become portfolio co-manager, sharing the management responsibility with a senior manager. The larger the pool of assets, the fiercer the competition.

What It Takes

There is no single prerequisite to becoming an asset manager. It all comes down to how much money you can make with other people's money. You don't need any professional licensing unless you're in a position to make buy and sell recommendations directly to a client (and employers will typically give you time and possibly even money to get any needed licenses if your job does include making recommendations to clients). That said, virtually all successful asset managers possess the following skills:

Quantitative and analytical skills. Asset managers have to be able to read spreadsheets and earnings reports. And they have to be able to take those numbers and crunch them into financial models and future projections. Even if you're dealing with less volatile investments such as bonds or real estate, you have to do the math to stay ahead of conventional wisdom. Classes in accounting and statistics are a big help, as are jobs that require number crunching, from I-banking to management consulting.

Managerial and organizational skills. Whether you're a researcher or a fund manager, you'll have to keep track of reams of facts to glean the really important information. Furthermore, you'll have to be able to make decisions—and execute them—quickly and accurately. Delay can cost big money. Finally, you need to be able to motivate and manage a talented staff of researchers and analysts if you work your way up to portfolio manager. Without their coordinated efforts, you may not have the information you need to make the best decision possible. "Solid general management experience is always in demand," says a recruiter. "There is such an opportunity for financial success without managing people at all that many professionals don't do it, don't want it, and don't develop the skills."

The Odds: Fair

There are lots and lots of different kinds of funds available, and the number is growing all the time. Which means there's a need for lots and lots of fund managers. Even if you don't make it to fund manager in the company you go to work for, as a buy-side analyst you'll be gaining skills that will make you highly attractive to other financial firms—and if you have an entrepreneurial bent, you'll be well-equipped to start your own fund some day.

ADDITIONAL RESOURCES

Careers in Asset Management and Retail Brokerage (WetFeet Insider Guide, available from www.WetFeet.com)

The Hedge Fund Association (www.thehfa.org)

Institutional Investor (www.institutionalinvestor.com)

Morningstar (www.morningstar.com)

Pensions and Investments (www.pionline.com)

PROFILE

John Calamos, Portfolio Manager

John Calamos is the 60-something CEO and chief investment officer of Calamos Asset Management, which he runs with his nephew, Nick Calamos. When he was a teenager, he convinced his parents, penny-pinching Greek immigrants to the United States, to give him $5,000 to invest. Some of the stock he bought tanked, but others performed well, and in 1977, when he founded Calamos Asset Management, his parents and other relatives were among the new company's first clients.

 CALAMOS ON HIS MILLION DOLLAR CAREER

Calamos describes his approach to portfolio management:

"We do a lot of quantitative modeling from the total universe of stocks. We're downloading data every day, looking at different trends using various models. Once that's done, we backfill that with qualitative data and balance-sheet items."

(from an interview with TheStreet.com)

Calamos Asset Management differentiates itself from most of its competition via its expertise in convertible-bond investments. (Convertible bonds are corporate bonds that can be converted to shares of company stock. Today, U.S. companies issue some $70 billion in convertible debt each year.) Calamos Asset Management has used its expertise in investing in convertibles to return some of the more impressive fund returns in the industry in recent years.

Calamos studied economics as an undergraduate at the Illinois Institute of Technology, where he also got an MBA in finance. He joined the Air Force after finishing school, becoming a combat pilot and eventually earning the rank of Major during the Vietnam War. In addition to running his company, Calamos speaks at industry events, appears on investing-related TV shows, and writes investment-related books. Calamos Asset Management currently has some $38 billion under management. In 2004, Calamos brought the company public, raising $414 million in the process. In 2003, the most recent year for which figures are available, John Calamos's compensation was in excess of $3.3 million.

Chief Executive Officer

WHAT YOU CAN MAKE

CEOs can make bank—big-time. Want proof? Here's a look at what the 25 best-compensated CEOs made in 2004.

Rank	CEO	Company	Compensation ($M)
1	Terry S. Semel	Yahoo!	230.6
2	Barry Diller	IAC/InterActiveCorp	156.2
3	William W. McGuire	UnitedHealth Group	124.8
4	Howard Solomon	Forest Laboratories	92.1
5	George David	United Technologies	88.7
6	Lew Frankfort	Coach	86.5
7	Edwin M. Crawford	Caremark Rx	77.9
8	Ray R. Irani	Occidental Petroleum	64.1
9	Angelo R. Mozilo	Countrywide Financial	57.0
10	Richard D. Fairbank	Capital One Financial	56.7
11	C. John Wilder	TXU	54.9
12	Richard M. Kovacevich	Wells Fargo	53.1
13	Robert I. Toll	Toll Brothers	50.2
14	Lawrence J. Ellison	Oracle	45.8
15	William E. Greehey	Valero Energy	44.9
16	Irwin M. Jacobs	Qualcomm	44.4
17	Rodney B. Mott	International Steel Group	42.7
18	John T. Chambers	Cisco Systems	40.2
19	Richard S. Fuld Jr.	Lehman Brothers	40.1
20	Bruce E. Karatz	KB Home	38.8
21	Jerry A. Grundhofer	U.S. Bancorp	38.6

Rank	CEO	Company	Compensation ($M)
22	Kevin B. Rollins	Dell	38.5
23	Bob R. Simpson	XTO Energy	38.3
24	Dwight C. Schar	NVR	38.2
25	James R. Tobin	Boston Scientific	38.1

Source: CEO Compensation, *Forbes*, 4/21/05.

And, according to a *Forbes* report, in 2004 CEOs at America's 500 largest companies received average compensation of $5.1 million. A pretty penny, indeed. Part of the reason CEOs today make so much, of course, is that they typically receive significant chunks of equity in their companies as part of their compensation.

JOB DESCRIPTION

A CEO is the highest-ranking manager in a company. Most are offered near-total autonomy in handling the day-to-day affairs of their organizations. All staff members work under their authority.

CEOs of publicly traded companies must answer to a board of directors. The board sets the standards by which a CEO must live. Board members can order a CEO's dismissal if they feel that he or she is not meeting the objectives they've set.

A CEO has to have a clear vision for the future of the company, and then express that plan to employees, shareholders, and business partners, inspiring them all with confidence. CEOs must be able to raise money by getting venture capitalists to buy into their dreams or by getting Wall Street to underwrite a bond offering worth hundreds of millions of dollars. When necessary, CEOs will ruffle feathers. They know how to get things done and are willing to do whatever it takes.

Some CEOs are more involved in their companies than others. In small organizations, the CEO may be part of day-to-day operations. Other CEOs concentrate on promoting their companies by giving speeches, attending trade shows, cultivating the press, and acting as evangelists for their companies. They leave the direct management work to the president and general manager.

Long hours and extended travel are expected. Many CEOs are on the road more than 90 percent of the time, visiting national and international offices, attending meetings and conferences sponsored by associations, monitoring operations, meeting with customers, and attending trade shows. In the book *Gig* (Crown Publishers, 2000), Robert Devlin, CEO of American General Corporation, says, "I'm often working eighteen-hour days. I rarely get more than four or five hours a night of sleep. And the way I view it, and I tell the guys, my senior staff, you know, these are seven-day-a-week, twenty-four-hours-a-day jobs."

Finally, as a result of the accounting and corporate scandals of the early 2000s, and the Sarbanes-Oxley legislation that resulted, today CEOs at public companies are required to sign off on their companies' accounting statements, to verify their accuracy and to show they'll be accountable should those accounting statements turn out to be fraudulent.

MAKING IT

Typical Career Paths

There is no completely typical path to the CEO level. Some CEOs have worked for their company for their entire careers. Others had careers as investment bankers or management consultants before becoming executives in industry. Some have MBAs or other advanced degrees; others don't even have college degrees. CEOs can have a wide range of professional backgrounds, but usually have a background in a function that's of core importance to a given company. In other words, in the consumer packaged goods industry, where branding efforts are of paramount importance, CEOs typically have consumer brand marketing backgrounds. In the semiconductor industry, on the other hand, you'll find many more CEOs with engineering backgrounds. The one function that seems to breed CEOs regardless of industry is finance, since the bottom line is of paramount importance in any kind of business venture.

Another way to become CEO, it's important to note, is to start an entrepreneurial venture. Start-up founders often take on the CEO mantle. Often, though, as their companies grow and become more complex, these CEOs are forced by investors or by good sense to relinquish the CEO role to someone more experienced running a growing, complex company.

What It Takes

There are no formal requirements for CEOs. Some have MBAs; others don't. The requirements for CEOs include leadership ability, communication skills, a deep understanding of the company and the industry in which it competes, the ability to forge good relationships with the press and investors, and the ability to see beyond the nitty-gritty of what's happening day-to-day in the business and think strategically about what the company should do to maximize profits over time.

I'm often working eighteen-hour days. I rarely get more than four or five hours a night of sleep.

Successful general managers have a variety of styles. Some are charismatic leaders who inspire their employees to reach their highest potential. Others are excellent behind-the-scenes operators who delegate authority to their managers. Most successful general managers have developed strong written and oral communication skills, the ability to make others feel at ease, and a strong, focused sense of purpose. Furthermore, they know how to get things done and aren't afraid to rock the boat to do so.

The Odds: Poor

Among the Fortune 500, which employ millions of people—including many thousands who probably have or could gain the skills necessary to be CEOs—there are only (you guessed it!) 500 CEOs. That's not a very promising ratio.

The good thing is that if you aspire to be a CEO, and you work hard and excel in your career, even if you don't ever attain your goal, you'll still enjoy a high-powered career as a business executive.

ADDITIONAL RESOURCES

Chief Executive (www.chiefexecutive.net)

Forbes (www.forbes.com)

Fortune (www.fortune.com)

The McKinsey Quarterly (www.mckinseyquarterly.com)

PROFILE

Carly Fiorina, CEO

Until early 2005, Carly Fiorina was CEO of Hewlett-Packard, a major manufacturer of technology products. She joined HP as CEO in 1999, where for a number of years she was a media darling. But there were problems at HP, and the cracks really began to show when Fiorina pushed to merge with rival Compaq. The company became divided down the middle by the merger, with Fiorina and her supporters on one side and members of the founders' families on the other. When HP stock underperformed after the Compaq merger was complete, the board forced Fiorina out of her position.

Fiorina came to HP from Lucent, where she was a hot-shot executive during the tech boom of the late 1990s. She was born in 1954 in Austin, Texas, went to Stanford for college, and got an MBA from the University of Maryland and an MS in management from MIT's Sloan School of Management.

As part of her severance agreement with HP, Fiorina will receive $14 million in cash. She'll also get more than $7 million in performance bonuses, and her total severance package could be worth $42 million. Not bad for someone who's just been fired.

 FIORINA'S ADVICE

In her commencement speech to Stanford graduates in 2001, Fiorina offered the following guidance:

"Let your fear motivate you, not inhibit you. Ask yourself the tough questions: Am I acting out a role, or am I living the truth? Am I still making choices, or have I simply stopped choosing? Am I in a place that engages my mind and captures my heart? Am I stuck in the past, or am I defining my future?

Chief Financial Officer

WHAT YOU CAN MAKE

CFOs at Fortune 500 companies typically make $500,000 to $1 million per year or more. Even at smaller companies, CFOs can make several hundred thousand dollars per year. That's a nice chunk of change.

JOB DESCRIPTION

The CFO is responsible for managing and analyzing all the financial resources of an organization. The CFO oversees the financial details of the company, from the micro level (e.g., making sure sales are booked accurately) to the macro level (e.g., setting budgets for all the departments of the company). He or she keeps track of the bank's finances, overseeing the P&L (short for profit and loss) and balance sheet for everything from individual product lines to the company as a whole. The CFO works with the CEO and other senior executives to plan and implement strategies that the executive teams deem essential to future success for the company. He or she advises senior management on the financial state and performance of all the areas of the company, as well as on ways to lower costs, manage risk, and increase financial performance, and forecasts financial performance and budgetary needs. The CFO also delivers information to external entities such as shareholders, creditors, tax authorities, regulatory authorities, and the bank's auditors. And the CFO reinvests corporate profits in safe, but lucrative, business or investment opportunities. Some other possible responsibilities include raising capital to help grow the business, managing the acquisition of or merger with other businesses, overseeing the initial public offering of the company, and analyzing changing tax laws.

Hmm, no wonder the CFO is paid so handsomely.

MAKING IT

Typical Career Paths

CFOs typically begin their careers in entry-level finance or accounting positions, in a corporation's accounting or finance department or at a public accounting firm. Most get their CPA designation somewhere along the way; some get an MBA, sometimes in addition to their CPA. Regardless of where they start their career, they end up working in industry at some point, moving up the finance-department ladder over time. When a company needs a new CFO, it will either hire a high-performing finance manager from within or look outside the company for candidates who either already have CFO experience or are finance professionals ready to step up to the CFO level.

What It Takes

First of all, the CFO needs to understand finance in and out; the language and logic of finance need to be second nature to anyone at this level. Often, a CPA, an MBA, or both will be required of candidates for CFO openings.

The CFO also needs a deep understanding of the business in which he or she works, both in terms of what happens in the company and the industry day-to-day and in terms of broad trends in the industry (and the business opportunities that may arise as a result of those trends). Similarly, the CFO needs to be able to think strategically—to think beyond day-to-day concerns to help shape the company to be better prepared for future challenges and opportunities.

The CFO also needs to be a strong communicator. The CFO is the finance expert among the senior executive staff at his or her company, after all, and must be able to communicate his or her thoughts about the financial impact of various strategies and tactics to the rest of the senior executives, so that the decisions they make together are as well-thought-out as they can be. Communication skills are handy for the CFO when it comes time to interact with the press and with the investment community.

As the head of the finance department, the CFO needs to be a good leader and manager. The efficiency and quality of work of that key department is the CFO's responsibility, after all.

Finally, in these days of increased attention to corporate malfeasance, the CFO needs to have a strong attention to detail and a strong sense of ethics. The CFO is in a key position to prevent accounting fraud and other unethical corporate behavior.

The Odds: Fair

The odds of making it to the CFO level are better than those of making it to the CEO level in corporate America. The reason? Professionals from all corporate functions aim to become CEOs; CFOs, on the other hand, are finance and accounting professionals, which means there's a smaller pool of folks vying for CFO positions than CEO positions.

Possible promotion opportunities for CFOs include becoming a COO, CEO, or president. Those who don't make it all the way to the CFO probably won't be getting mega-wealthy any time soon, but can usually enjoy nice, solid careers in corporate finance or accounting departments, as directors or managers, for instance.

ADDITIONAL RESOURCES

CareerJournal.com's Corporate Finance page (www.careerjournal.com/salaryhiring/industries/corpfinance/index.html)

Careers in Accounting (WetFeet Insider Guide, available from www.WetFeet.com)

CFO magazine (www.cfo.com)

Financial Executives International (www.fei.org)

PROFILE

Susan Decker, CFO and EVP of Finance and Administration

Susan Decker has been CFO of Yahoo! since 2000. Unlike many CFOs, Decker did not work her way up through the ranks of corporate America's finance departments. Rather, she had a long and successful career as an investment banking research analyst, working for 14 years at Donaldson, Lufkin & Jenrette in San Francisco, and making her fair share of notable-Wall-Street-analysts lists in the process. At DLJ, she covered media, publishing, and advertising companies. With her knowledge of Yahoo!'s industry and business and her own financial prowess, Decker was a natural fit for the Yahoo! CFO position, despite her nontraditional career path (for a CFO, that is).

According to the Yahoo! website, Decker "is a key participant in determining Yahoo!'s business strategy, and is also responsible for managing and setting all aspects of the company's financial and administrative direction within key functional areas, including finance, human resources, legal, and investor relations."

Decker did her undergraduate studies at Tufts, outside Boston, and got her MBA at Harvard. She also has a CFA designation. In 2004, she received a salary of $1.4 million. But the real financial windfall for her during the year came in the form of exercised stock options: She exercised options worth $27.7 million in 2004. Yahoo! indeed.

Consulting Firm Principal

WHAT YOU CAN MAKE

Annual salaries for consulting firm partners start at about $250,000, and if you're a principal (partner) at a big successful consulting firm—a McKinsey or Accenture or Booz Allen Hamilton—you can make well into the six figures each year, depending on your firm's performance.

JOB DESCRIPTION

Management consultants advise corporations and other organizations regarding an infinite array of business issues—everything from new-product launches and mergers and acquisitions to personnel issues and IT strategies and tactics.

Research and analysis are the main tools of the trade for management consultants. They analyze a business problem from various angles by conducting research and forming and testing hypotheses. Research may consist of collecting raw data from internal sources—such as the client's computers or employees—and external sources, such as trade associations or government agencies. Consultants get some of their most valuable data from surveys and market studies that they devise and implement themselves. The data must then be analyzed in relation to the client's organization, operations, customers, and competitors to locate potential areas for improvement and form solutions. These solutions are then recommended to the client and—hopefully—implemented. (Sometimes convincing a client to accept a consultant's recommendations can be the most difficult aspect of the job, and there is always a chance that the client will choose not to accept the consultant's recommendation at all.)

Consulting firm professionals typically make it to principal after 5 to 10 years in the field. By this point, they're experts in their industry of focus or practice area (e.g., change management, or strategy, or IT); in many cases, as a principal, they are responsible for running an entire practice area for a firm. They oversee a number of different client engagements at the same time; the consulting managers in charge of those individual clients report to the principal. They're also usually very involved in staff training and development.

For most principals, business development is a big part of the job. Principals have extensive interactions with senior executives at client organizations about current and possible future engagements; fostering those relationships is a major factor in a principal's success in winning new business for his or her firm.

Like most management consulting professionals, depending on the location of the clients they're serving, principals can spend a lot of time traveling to and from client sites.

 ORIT GADIESH ON CONSULTING SUCCESS

In an interview with the Harvard Business School, Orit Gadiesh offered her take on what it takes to succeed in management consulting:

"You should be able to focus on one or two things and be extremely good at them but if you lose your curiosity about other things you're not going to be good even in the few things you focus on. You'll be much too narrow minded or much too narrowly focused."

"I think a big part of what consulting does has to do with psychology and learning to really listen to what people are saying both verbally and nonverbally."

MAKING IT

Typical Career Paths

While midcareer professionals with deep industry knowledge do often move to consulting
careers, most professionals at management consulting firms begin their consulting career at an
earlier stage than that. Undergrads join consulting firms as analysts. After a couple of years,
most leave their firm to enter another field or
get their MBA; there are few exceptions to this.

> **Above all, you need inter-
> personal skills because in
> the end, this is a sales job. You
> have to be able to sell your
> ideas to clients, or all of the
> work that you did in formulat-
> ing the ideas means nothing.**

Whether they have analyst experience or not, MBAs typically join management consulting firms as associate consultants. The exact titles and number of steps between
associate and principal vary from firm to firm, but in general, associates are eventually
promoted to manager, and managers are eventually promoted to principal.

What It Takes

In most cases, it's next to impossible to become a principal at a major management
consulting firm without an MBA. Beyond that requirement, specialists in various fields
may have industry certification; for example, an IT consultant may have one or more
technology certifications.

Management consultants need strong analytical skills, especially the ability to look at a
client organization and determine what's not working or could be improved. They need
good problem-solving skills, to be able to suggest solutions to those problems or areas of
potential improvement. They need to have a service orientation—their careers are built
on serving their clients, after all—and they need to be willing and able to put in long
hours serving those clients. They need good people skills and good communication and

presentation skills. And they need a deep and sincere interest in business and the curiosity to stay on top of what's happening in the business world and among consultants.

An insider sums it up as follows: "You must have strong analytical skills. Quantitative skills especially are a big asset, as there is less of a need in consulting for purely qualitative analysis. You must like to learn and work hard and be able to think fast. Above all, though, you need interpersonal skills—especially with clients—because in the end, this is a sales job. You have to be able to sell your ideas to clients, or all of the work that you did in formulating the ideas means nothing."

The Odds: Poor

Very few professionals even get their feet in the door at the top-notch management consulting firms in the first place—and the bulk of those were the best of the best in the Ivy League and schools of similarly impressive reputation. For most people, consulting serves as a professional training ground—it's a weigh station on the way to their "real" career in business. And for good reason—only a small number of those who go into consulting make it to principal.

ADDITIONAL RESOURCES

Ace Your Case! series of consulting case interview guides
(available from www.WetFeet.com)

CareerJournal.com's Consulting page (www.careerjournal.com/salaryhiring/industries/consulting/index.html)

Careers in Management Consulting (WetFeet Insider Guide, available from www.WetFeet.com)

Kennedy Information's Consulting Central (www.consultingcentral.com)

Killer Consulting Resumes! (WetFeet Insider Guide, available from www.WetFeet.com)

PROFILE

Orit Gadiesh, Consulting Firm Partner and Chairperson

Orit Gadiesh joined Bain & Company, the hot-shot management consulting firm formed just a few years earlier by ex–Boston Consulting Group consultant Bill Bain, in 1977, after finishing her MBA at Harvard Business School. By 1982, she was a vice president at the firm. When the firm faced financial crisis in the early 1990s, she spearheaded the effort to get Bain back on its feet, dramatically boosting morale at the firm in the process. In 1993, her importance to Bain was formally recognized when the firm named her its first chairperson—a position whose responsibilities primarily comprise client work.

Gadiesh is originally from Israel, where she was a military intelligence officer and then got her undergraduate degree from Hebrew University. She then went to Harvard Business School, where she excelled. In her early days at Bain, she focused on working for steel-industry clients. Despite resistance from some in the old-school, old-boys' industry (one executive once told her that women were considered "bad luck" in steel plants), she succeeded in helping clients implement innovative solutions to their business problems.

Her independent, no-one-can-tell-me-how-to-live style—even though she works in the relatively buttoned-up, Ivy-bred management consulting industry, for a long time she wore her hair tinted a garish purple—has helped her become the leader she is, and, according to *Forbes* magazine, one of the 100 most powerful women in business.

Entrepreneur

WHAT YOU CAN MAKE

The sky's the limit for entrepreneurs. Take some of the biggest entrepreneurial success stories of the past few decades. Jeff Bezos and Amazon.com, for instance. Or Michael Dell and his Dell Inc. Or Jerry Yang and Yahoo! Or Steve Jobs and Apple Computer, or Bill Gates and Microsoft. One thing all these entrepreneurs have in common: Thanks to the success of the companies they founded, they're now among the 100 richest Americans alive.

JOB DESCRIPTION

An entrepreneur is the business version of someone who builds something new where there was nothing before. Today some people only use the term *entrepreneur* to refer to someone who founds a technology-related start-up, but that's not an accurate use of the word. Consider Sam Walton, the founder of Wal-Mart, who, early in his career, owned a number of franchises of another retailer. When he realized that a store that sold only discount goods would succeed in the marketplace, like any true entrepreneur, he started Wal-Mart.

The responsibilities of an entrepreneur are many and diverse. To get a new business up and running, the founder may have to be involved in everything from studying the marketplace to looking for business opportunities, creating the new company's business plan, and raising the capital needed to start the business to hiring staff, marketing the new company and its products, and managing the day-to-day operations of the company. No matter what industry her company is in, the entrepreneur has to wear a variety of hats. One hour, she might be interviewing potential new employees to help build her business. The next, she may be thinking through strategy for a new business plan to attract new investment. If a customer calls, she may have to put on her sales or customer service hat. Or, if the business needs supplies or services, she may have to deal with business vendors such as phone-service providers and raw-materials suppliers. If the business is growing in terms of staff or production-facility needs, she may have to go check out potential new locations with a real estate broker. She may be involved in packing and shipping products, going to industry functions to network with potential clients and business partners, doing interviews with the business press to get the word out about her company and its offerings, researching competitors in the marketplace, writing press releases, speaking at conferences, reviewing sales and cost figures with her accountant, creating new product packaging . . . the list of potential responsibilities for entrepreneurs goes on and on and on.

MAKING IT

Typical Career Paths

There is no typical career path for entrepreneurs. There are all kinds of stories of successful entrepreneurs—from students who start a new business out of their parents' garage to older folks who decide to turn an old family recipe for spaghetti sauce into a new food business. Often, though, entrepreneurs start new ventures in the same industry in which they've already worked or in which they're students or professors. Sam Walton is one example. Herbert Boyer, the molecular biologist who, with venture capitalist Robert Swenson, started Genentech in 1976, is another. Sergey Brin and Larry Page are two more examples; these Stanford computer-science graduate students started Google in 1999.

Entrepreneurs need money to start their businesses. For many new small businesses, this money comes from personal savings; small-business founders may also turn to banks for small-business loans to get their businesses going.

Ventures based on advanced technologies, on the other hand (everything from computer software companies and e-commerce ventures to medical technology companies and biotech concerns), often turn to investors to raise capital. Early on in a company's life, this can mean "angel" investors—often wealthy individuals who give start-up companies "seed" capital. After the business shows real signs of succeeding, this usually means venture capitalists, who often demand to have a major say in the direction of the company as a condition of making an investment in it.

 IN IT FOR THE MONEY?

Sheldon Laube, founder of both CenterBeam and USWeb, on who is likely to succeed as an entrepreneur:

"People who want to build things. No great entrepreneur is in it for the money. They're in it because they love it. Bill Gates and Larry Ellison don't go to work thinking about the money they are making—they go there because they have a passion for their business."

What It Takes

There are typically no formal requirements for entrepreneurs. Those who do well are often single-minded in their pursuit of success for their new venture. The entrepreneur needs to have a good head for business, in order to spot opportunities in the marketplace and to create a strong business plan to attract the capital needed to get the business on its feet. The entrepreneur needs to have a good eye for talent in other people, since the staff he hires to get his company up and running will be a major factor in whether it succeeds or fails. The entrepreneur needs to be a good communicator and a good leader, so as to be able to make others (everyone from bankers or investors to staff) see the possibilities in his or her vision. The entrepreneur must have a knack for building relationships with others, from potential investors to the customers of the new company (since a happy customer is a repeat customer—and one who'll spread the word about the entrepreneur's business to friends). And perhaps more important than anything else, the entrepreneur has to be driven to do whatever it takes to achieve success for the business; successful entrepreneurs are notorious for working ridiculously long, hard hours.

Many experienced entrepreneurs point out that plenty of successful entrepreneurs also have a failed business venture ot two in their past, and these failures can be an asset. As W. Wyatt Stearns, founder of Tripwire Security Systems, puts it: "You have to manage your fear. If you worry too much about failing, you will. Investors, employees, partners—can all smell fear, and they'll bolt. That's why it's often helpful to have one or two failures under your belt, so you know it's not the end of the world. Having faced your greatest fear helps you manage it in the future."

For those who want to start VC-backed companies, it is a major help to have gone to school, either as an undergrad or (preferably) to get an MBA, at a top-flight school such as Stanford or Harvard. The reason for this is that a large percentage of the VC community comes from schools like these, and it can be much easier to get VCs' attention if you (or, at least, members of the management team you've hired to help run your start-up) can readily tap into this network of movers and shakers.

Entrepreneurs also need to know when to step aside—when their company has gotten too big or is growing too fast for them to be the best person to make decisions about its future. Consider a hypothetical tech start-up founded by a couple of kids right out of college. These kids have a great idea, and they work hard at building their new technology. At a certain point, though—when it comes time to ramp up sales of their product, say, or raise money from venture capitalists—these kids may be smart to bring in some seasoned professionals to help take their company to the next level of success. Consider Larry Page and Sergey Brin, the computer-geek founders of Google, who, as their company grew, gave key executive jobs to more industry-savvy pros—like CEO Eric Schmidt, formerly of Novell and Sun Microsystems.

The Odds: Fair

For the right kind of person, the odds are better than fair. A hard-core entrepreneur may start several failed business ventures before coming up with a business that sticks, but the chances of ultimate success for someone so driven are pretty good. For many would-be entrepreneurs, on the other hand, the risks of starting a new business (giving up the security of a steady income, for instance) outweigh the possible benefits; they'll only become entrepreneurs given just the right business opportunity. And even the best new-business ideas can fail: According to the U.S. Bureau of Labor Statistics, 44 percent of new businesses close within the first 2 years.

 ON THE ROLE OF FAILURE

W. Wyatt Stearns describes the path to entrepreneurial success as follows:

"Most entrepreneurs have four or five previous experiences under their belt—and not all of them successful ones. The ones who will succeed overall are the ones who just refuse to quit. Success is never a straight line. Crash and burn is still more the rule than the exception. To be an entrepreneur you need to have a blend of persistence and vision. You need to be smart enough to get your message across to others, but dumb enough to just keep plugging even when the odds may seem against you."

ADDITIONAL RESOURCES

Entrepreneur magazine (www.entrepreneur.com)

EntreWorld: resources for entrepreneurs (www.entreworld.org)

Garage.com

Harvard Business School's series of entrepreneur profiles (www.hbs.edu/entrepreneurs)

Startup Journal (www.startupjournal.com)

U.S. Small Business Administration (www.sba.gov)

PROFILE

Richard Branson, Entrepreneur

If you ever meet Richard Branson, don't call him Mr. Branson. Call him Sir Branson. After all, this entrepreneur was knighted for his business exploits by the Queen of England, his home country, in 1999. A knightship isn't all he's earned from his entrepreneurial exploits, though; according to *Forbes*, his net worth is $3.2 billion.

Branson began his entrepreneurial ways in 1968, when he dropped out of school at 17 to run a magazine he'd created, called *Student*. Two years later, in 1970, he started Virgin, at first selling records by mail order, then opening physical store locations, then signing and recording major rock acts including the Sex Pistols, Culture Club, and the Rolling Stones. In 1984 Branson added to his portfolio of companies by founding Virgin Atlantic, an airline company. Branson sold the Virgin Music Group in 1992, but got back in the recording game in 1996, with the founding of the V2 record label. Other Branson ventures include Virgin Cola, a soft-drink company, and Virgin Mobile, a wireless-communications company. Branson's next big entrepreneurial venture is Virgin Galactic, which hopes to make flights to suborbital space available to the public in 2007.

 BRANSON ON HIS ENTREPRENEURIAL NATURE

"I'm inquisitive . . . and I love a new challenge . . . and if I feel that we can do it better than it's been done by other people, we'll have a go."
(*from an interview with* Foreign Correspondent*)*

An inveterate self-promoter, Branson gets a lot of attention for his long-distance hot air ballooning feats. He has crossed the Atlantic Ocean and the Pacific Ocean, but so far has not made it all the way around the world. Branson also recently hosted an American reality-television series, *The Rebel Billionaire*, promoting him and the Virgin brand.

Fashion Designer

WHAT YOU CAN MAKE

Most fashion designers work as part of design teams at apparel manufacturing companies, or at retail companies that manufacture their own private-label apparel. They're regular corporate Joes (and Josephines)—salaried employees. Very few achieve wealthy-international-star status. Still, the possibility is there. Just ask someone like Ralph Lauren, who's created an empire that returned a profit of $190 million (on $3.3 billion in revenue) in fiscal 2005. Considering that he owns some 90 percent of the company, that's a pretty healthy return—and that's not including his salary!

JOB DESCRIPTION

Big-time fashion designers typically have a varied set of responsibilities. They spend a good chunk of their time drawing designs, of course. Designing apparel and accessories involves sketching designs, deciding on colors, and cutting and sewing together fabrics to create samples.

World-famous designers rarely design entire product lines themselves, though. So they need to be able to manage other designers who take their design philosophy and sensibility and extend it to products that the bigwig designer may never even see.

Designers may also spend time choosing fabrics and other materials to be used in their designs, and dealing with textile manufacturers or distributors.

Finally, because they're dealing with the notably fickle world of fashion, designers have to stay on top of trends in the industry—reading industry publications, looking through *Vogue* and *Women's Wear Daily*, and going to fashion shows and other industry events.

Designers who work for themselves—as almost all the biggest-name designers do—have additional responsibilities that go along with being a businessperson/entrepreneur. These folks have to do everything from dealing with fabric suppliers and negotiating with production vendors to networking with retailers to get their designs in stores and collecting money from stores to which they've delivered their fashions.

MAKING IT

Typical Career Paths

Most fashion designers are formally trained, either at a college or university with a design program or at a 2- or 3-year fashion design school. Going to school is a great help in putting together a strong portfolio, which is usually necessary to get a job in the field.

Most aspiring fashion designers start their working careers as design assistants for more recognized designers or mass-market apparel companies. According to Vera Wang (in a interview with *20/20* magazine), aspiring designers should look on this period of their career as an opportunity: "Don't be afraid to take time to learn. It's good to work for other people. I worked for others for 20 years. They paid me to learn." Eventually, they are either given the opportunity to take the design lead on some new products, or they begin designing and selling products on their own. After that, it's up to the marketplace (usually, with the help of the arbiters of fashion, such as the big fashion magazines) to determine whether they make it big.

What It Takes

Good design marries style with function, so designers typically have to be as focused on functionality as they are on aesthetics.

There are no formal requirements for this career, although most designers have some formal training somewhere along the line. Beyond that, fashion designers need to be very creative, of course. They need to be driven to put in the long hours necessary to have a chance at success in this field. And they need to have a good sense of marketing, to get their name and the word about their products out into the marketplace effectively, and business in general, to be able to make intelligent decisions about money and building their design business.

The Odds: Poor

If you compare the number of people who enter the field to the number who strike it rich as fashion designers, you'll probably come to the conclusion that making it big in this field is even less likely than becoming a Hollywood leading man or lady for aspiring actors.

Fashion designers who decide to change careers often make good interior designers, graphic designers, fashion consultants, and costume designers for stage or screen.

ADDITIONAL RESOURCES

Council of Fashion Designers of America (www.cfda.com)

Fashion Net (www.fashion.net)

Fashion Windows (www.fashionwindows.com)

StyleCareer.com

Women's Wear Daily (www.wwd.com)

PROFILE

Kate Spade, Fashion Designer

Kate Spade is the founder of her eponymous luxury-brand company, Kate Spade. She got into fashion when, after returning broke from a postcollege trip to Europe, she crashed at a New York friend's place and got a temp job in the fashion department at *Mademoiselle* magazine. She stayed at *Mademoiselle* for 5 years, becoming a senior fashion editor.

Spade started Kate Spade in 1993, with the help of her husband, Andy Spade (big brother of film and TV actor David Spade—for those who are keeping track, that makes at least three million dollar careers in the Spade family, CEO Andy Spade, actor David Spade, and designer Kate Spade). (Kate and Andy met while both were enrolled at Arizona State University; they worked together in a clothing store in Phoenix.) Her handbags, in simple-but-funky shapes and bright colors, were an immediate hit. Despite her coolness among New York fashionistas, Kate Spade is a product of the Midwest; she grew up in Kansas City, Missouri.

Today Spade's company, which has moved beyond handbags and now manufactures other fashion accessories and housewares as well, has 25 stores globally, 16 of them in the United States. The company, which had $125 million in revenue in 2004, is now majority-owned by The Neiman Marcus Group.

 THE DEVIL IS IN THE DETAILS

Kate Spade on one of the reasons for her success:

"I'm really a details-oriented person. But it is exhausting. I've worn myself to the bone on the details."

(from an interview with Index Magazine*)*

Film/TV Producer

WHAT YOU CAN MAKE

Bette Davis once famously said, "I don't take the movies seriously, and anyone who does is in for a headache." But if you love TV and film, you may be willing to deal with that headache. And if you make a big success of your career, the size of your bank account can go a long way toward assuaging that headache. In 2004, for example, producer Jerry Bruckheimer earned $66 million. Not bad.

Some producers, especially TV producers, are paid a set rate or salary for their services. But the real money for producers results from situations in which they receive a percentage of their production's success.

JOB DESCRIPTION

The producer is kind of like the chief operating officer of a television or film production. It's the producer's job to get all the materials and people involved in the production where they should be, when they should be there. In other words, the producer is the person who makes sure the trains are running on time—figuratively speaking, of course.

The specific responsibilities of the producer can be many. He or she may select the script that will be produced and manage writers to rewrite that script to make it better or more marketable. The producer may arrange the financing for the production. The producer hires and manages the crew for the production. He or she may be involved in auditioning actors for roles in the production. He or she negotiates contracts and oversees the production budget. The producer creates the production schedule. Finally, he or she may be involved in promoting the movie or TV show that is the result of the production.

Megaproducer Jerry Bruckheimer (who's produced *American Gigolo, Flashdance, Beverly Hills Cop, Top Gun, Days of Thunder, The Rock,* and *Con Air,* among other films) summarizes the job of a film producer:

> What you try to do is—well, first, you try to get a good idea. Good characters. A good story. It might come from a book, a screenplay. *Top Gun* came from a magazine article. It might come from a guy walking into your office. Whatever. Good ideas are good ideas. When we get one, we option it, get the film rights to it. Then we get some money. Hire some writers. Get a script. Work on the script. Work on it some more. Do more work on it as the director gets involved, and the actors start getting involved. Everyone brings something to it. We have characters in mind and we try to take these characters on a journey. . . . I think my talent is just recognizing good ideas and recognizing talent. I've had enormous success picking people who have a real gift and then managing the process to get the *Armageddon*s, the *Top Gun*s, the *Beverly Hills Cop*s. . . . It's a ton of work. I'm at this twelve to sixteen hours a day. Seven days a week. (*Gig,* Crown Publishers, 2000)

MAKING IT

Typical Career Paths

Many producers start out as aspiring actors or writers. Those who make it big typically move to L.A. or New York, where they get employment doing film or TV studio or production company work and/or go to film or television school. Those working in production companies move up the ladder (or job-hop) to gain their first head-producer experience. Others become independent producers, spotting a good film or TV show idea, developing the idea, getting financing to produce the idea, and getting the actual production on its legs themselves. To make it really big, the producer will need to be involved in a very successful movie or TV show.

What It Takes

There are no formal requirements for TV and film producers—no formal tests that need to be passed or required formal school experience. That said, most producers have a BA. The real requirements for success in the field are more practical. The producer must understand how a TV show or film gets made, from concept development through shooting and editing, and must understand the technologies used in the production—cameras, lighting, editing suites, and so on.

The producer must also be expert at negotiation; in the process of producing a film, for instance, a producer may have to negotiate with everyone from the investors financing the film,

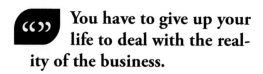 **You have to give up your life to deal with the reality of the business.**

to the actors he or she wants to appear in the film, to the studio where the bulk of the film is shot, to local governments or organizations on whose property the production needs to do location shooting, to the crew's union reps, to the studio that wants to distribute the finished film.

The producer must also be flexible, since it's the rare TV or film production that doesn't experience unexpected developments during production. The producer must have an extraordinary attention to detail to make sure those unexpected developments remain as rare as possible. The producer must be tireless in the pursuit of a quality finished product; as an insider says, "You have to give up your life to deal with the reality of the business." He or she must be a leader, so as to keep the production on track and moving forward at all times, as well as an independent self-starter. And the producer must have business acumen, so he or she can understand when moving a production forward is a good business proposition and when it'll mean throwing money away.

The Odds: Fair

The odds of making it as a producer are good. There are already some 75,000 producers working in the United States, and with the cost of producing a film or TV show falling (think: digital video—which is *much* cheaper than film—and reality programming, which eliminates most of the cost of employing talent), and the number of outlets for productions increasing (think: cable TV and the Internet), this number is sure to grow. The chances of making it really big, though, are somewhat more limited.

ADDITIONAL RESOURCES

Careers in Entertainment and Sports (WetFeet Insider Guide, available from www.WetFeet.com)

FilmLand (www.filmland.com)

The Hollywood Reporter (www.hollywoodreporter.com)

Variety (www.variety.com)

PROFILE

Harvey and Bob Weinstein, Film Producers

Many observers credit brothers Harvey and Bob Weinstein with changing Hollywood by spearheading the independent-film movement of the 1980s. But the Weinsteins did not start their careers in the entertainment industry producing films. Rather, in the 1970s, they produced concerts. Eventually, they did produce a film—a concert film—1979's *The Secret Policeman's Ball*. They used the money they earned from that job to start Miramax, the production company named after their parents (Max and Miriam) that would eventually propel them into the ranks of Hollywood's power elite.

Their first big success at Miramax was Errol Morris's 1988 documentary, *The Thin Blue Line*, about a wrongfully convicted death row prison inmate. That was followed in 1977 by *sex, lies, and videotape*, the film that put Steven Soderbergh on the map. More indie successes followed, until in 1993 Disney purchased Miramax for $80 million, in a deal that was even more notable for the amount of control the Weinsteins would continue to enjoy at Miramax than for the amount of money changing hands.

While part of Disney, Miramax has produced a slew of critically acclaimed, financially successful films, including *Pulp Fiction*, *The English Patient*, *Scream*, *Shakespeare in Love*, *Good Will Hunting*, *Chicago*, and *Fahrenheit 9/11*. But the relationship between Disney and the Weinsteins soured, and in 2005, the Weinsteins and Disney decided to part company. Disney is retaining the Miramax brand, but Harvey and Bob Weinstein will continue to produce movies via a production company with a name that's as yet to be determined. Disney is reportedly paying the brothers some $100 million as part of the deal.

Investment Banker

WHAT YOU CAN MAKE

In 2004, the typical investment banking managing director made in excess of $1.5 million. This is down from around $8 million back in 1995, but it's still pretty damn good money. And don't worry—if you're a superstar banker, you can end up making $10 million or more in a given year, depending on the value of the deals you work on and how much new business you land for your bank.

JOB DESCRIPTION

When you say "investment banker," most of us instantly have a mental image of the type. It involves expensive, yet conservative, business suits; penthouse apartments and multimillion-dollar homes in leafy suburbs; long, long hours at the office and jetting across the country; and business dinners that are not only at the best restaurants in town, but at which people regularly order the most expensive wines on the list. But what do investment bankers actually do?

Investment bankers help client companies in a variety of ways, primarily by helping them raise capital, advising them on financial strategies, and advising them when they're acquiring or merging with other companies or are themselves being acquired. Typically, investment bankers come in one of two flavors. Corporate finance bankers help clients raise capital via the issuance of securities like stocks or bonds. And mergers and acquisitions (M&A) bankers, of course, help clients who are involved in M&A activity.

The corporate finance group (frequently known as banking or CorpFin) serves the sellers of securities. These may be either Fortune 1000 companies that are looking to raise cash to fund growth or private companies that are looking to go public (i.e., to sell stock on the public markets for the first time). Think of investment bankers as financial consultants to corporations. This is where CEOs and CFOs turn when they're trying to figure out how to finance their operations, how to structure their balance sheets, or how best to move ahead with plans to sell or acquire a company. (M&A can also fall under the CorpFin umbrella, depending on the firm.)

The activities of the CorpFin department can range from providing pure financial advice to leading a company through its first equity issue (or IPO). As a result, industry or product

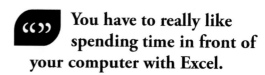

You have to really like spending time in front of your computer with Excel.

knowledge is key, and many investment banks divide their corporate finance departments into industry subgroups, such as technology, financial institutions, health care, communications, entertainment, utilities, and insurance, or into product groups like high-yield, private equity, and investment-grade debt.

The M&A group provides advice to companies that are buying another company or are themselves being acquired. M&A work can seem very glamorous and high profile. At the same time, the work leading up to the headline-grabbing multibillion-dollar acquisition can involve a Herculean effort to crunch all the numbers, perform the necessary due diligence, and work out the complicated structure of the deal. As one insider puts it, "You have to really like spending time in front of your computer with Excel." Often, the M&A team will also work with a CorpFin industry group to arrange the appropriate financing for the transaction (usually a debt or equity offering). In many cases, all this may happen on a very tight timeline and under extreme secrecy. M&A is often a subgroup within corporate finance; but in some firms, it is a stand-alone department. M&A can be one of the most demanding groups to work for.

In terms of being a million dollar career, investment banking is different from many of the other occupations in this guide in that it can be extraordinarily lucrative even if you don't have an equity position in your company—in other words, the help can get

> **Anyone can learn the technical skills like accounting and modeling. It's not so easy to learn how to be driven and to take responsibility, to own the deal.**

rich in investment banking, not just the owners. Nonpartners at investment banks can make millions of dollars in a single year. There are a couple of reasons for this. First, banks tend to share the wealth via employee bonuses when times are good. Second, if you bring in significant business to your firm, your bonus is going to be even bigger as a result. It's not at all unheard of for bankers to receive an annual bonus that's at least as big as their annual salaries. When you're talking about salaries of several hundred thousand dollars, that can translate to very meaningful *dinero*.

MAKING IT

Typical Career Paths

The typical investment banking career begins in college, when the aspiring banker makes sure to major in business or economics or another of the quantitative fields (engineering, perhaps, or math) that banks find so sexy. It continues with a summer internship, followed by a full-time analyst position. After a couple of years, the young investment banker goes back to school to get an MBA. After 2 years of B-school, which include a summer associate position in investment banking, the banker returns to the business and tries to work on important (read: big-money) deals while moving up the ladder within the bank or by accepting job offers from competing banks.

What It Takes

Investment bankers need an undergraduate degree, in most cases from a top-notch school. Most investment bankers will also need an MBA to advance to higher levels in the industry. That's pretty much it in terms of formal requirements. However, the informal job requirements can be myriad, and include the right kind (read: analytical, quant-based) coursework while in school; a polished, professional mien; an ability to work very hard (for relatively little money, at least early in one's career); and a hunger to make money for one's self and one's employer.

Investment banking jobs like corporate finance require critical, detail-oriented thinking. If you have a knack for using numbers to understand patterns that influence business, you're going to be valuable to a company. If you can't crunch and analyze them, this isn't going to be the right job for you. You should also enjoy and excel at solving problems and be able to think critically about the numbers you're working with.

Investment bankers also need excellent people skills and communication skills, both to work on banking teams and to build solid relationships with clients.

Lawyers can make as good a fit in this career as MBAs, and experienced candidates with strong experience in a given industry make good candidates for investment banking positions.

Beyond all that, success in this career requires tremendous drive. "Anyone can learn the technical skills like accounting and modeling," says one insider. "It's not so easy to learn how to be driven and to take responsibility, to own the deal." But for many in investment banking, the promise of big bucks is all the carrot they need each morning.

The Odds: Fair

The toughest part of the journey for many who make it to the top in investment banking is getting in the door in the first place. This industry is notoriously picky when it comes to hiring entry-level employees. If you're not at the top of your class, or at a top college or university, you probably won't even get an interview at the top investment banks, whether you're an undergrad or an MBA candidate. Even among those who do get in the door, the attrition level is high; many people leave investment banking after their 2-year analyst stints, having learned that the culture, the business, or the pace of the work isn't right for them.

Still, if you can get that first job in investment banking, do well in it, go to business school, then perform well for your bank after you're an associate, when compared with other industries and careers, in investment banking the odds are good that you'll be making well into the six figures in a relatively short time.

Note that getting in the door via internships is an excellent strategy if you want a career as an investment banker; undergrads and MBAs both should pursue this option, as interns have a real advantage over other applicants when it comes time for banks to hire full-time employees.

If you ever decide to leave investment banking, many of the skills you've learned will be in great demand in other industries and careers. For instance, negotiating skills can come in handy in business development jobs. And your understanding of finance will be attractive to all kinds of companies across industries.

ADDITIONAL RESOURCES

Beat the Street series of investment banking interview guides (WetFeet Insider Guides, available from www.WetFeet.com)

Careers in Investment Banking (WetFeet Insider Guide, available from www.WetFeet.com)

InvestorLinks.com

Investor's Business Daily (www.investors.com)

Killer Investment Banking Resumes! (WetFeet Insider Guide, available from www.WetFeet.com)

PROFILE

Bruce Wasserstein, Investment Banker

To artsy types, Bruce Wasserstein is probably best known for being the brother of play-write Wendy Wasserstein. But to those with any kind of awareness of the business world, he's a legend—an investment banking dealmaker extraordinaire, who's helped broker more than 1,000 corporate transactions worth in excess of $250 billion since the 1980s. Indeed, Wasserstein has played a huge role in making M&A banking and merchant banking the vibrant banking sectors they are today; his deal-making showed bankers just how much potential there was in both activities and helped create the M&A boom of the 1980s.

After going to the University of Michigan as an undergrad, then on to complete both business school and law school at Harvard, Wasserstein began his career as an attorney with the big New York law firm Cravath, Swaine & Moore. But he left the practice of law to become a banker for First Boston, where he rose to become co-head of invest-ment banking. Next, starting in 1988, he co-founded and served as CEO of the M&A house Wasserstein Perella Group, which Dresdner Bank purchased at the stock market peak in 2001. He then worked for less than a year at Dresdner Kleinwort Wasserstein before becoming CEO of Lazard, the last big partnership on Wall Street, in 2002. In 2005, Wasserstein wrested control of Lazard from its European controlling interests, taking the firm public and making himself about $292 million in the process. (This is in addition to the $3 million salary he took home in 2004.)

During his career, "Bid-'em-up Bruce" (the nickname comes from his reputation for getting the maximum possible financial return from the deals he's involved in) has worked on notable corporate transactions including the merger of Morgan Stanley and Dean Witter; UBS's acquisition of Paine Webber; the merger of AOL and Time Warner; Philip Morris's acquisitions of General Foods, Kraft, and Nabisco; the merger of Beecham and SmithKline; Capital Cities' acquisition of ABC; and Standard Oil's sale to British Petroleum.

Investment Bank Sales and Trading

WHAT YOU CAN MAKE

Salespeople and traders working at investment banks typically earn a salary (a nice, healthy salary), but they make their real money in commissions and bonuses. In a good year (one in which investors are actively investing), a salesperson or trader with strong skills and a good book of clients can easily make $1 million.

JOB DESCRIPTION

You can think of sales and trading as being similar to the sales force for any corporation. This group is responsible for selling all of the financial products (stocks, bonds, and their derivatives) sponsored by the investment banking department. As such, it is the vital link between the sellers (corporations and government entities) and the buyers (investors). Depending on the firm, the buyers may be institutions (pension funds, mutual funds, insurance companies, hedge funds, and other asset managers), high-net-worth individuals, or private investors. Although frequently lumped together, salespeople and traders actually perform different functions.

Sales

An investment bank's sales professionals typically have a list of institutional clients to whom they pitch new offerings, offer portfolio management advice, and sell securities. The sales department may be divided by account size, security type (debt or equity), geography, or product line. The department is typically divided into large institutional, middle market, and retail (or private-client services) sections. In other words, a salesperson who manages a high-volume institutional account would not likely handle a smaller, low-volume buyer as well. Groups may be further divided based on the complexity of a bank's financial products, such as government securities, corporate securities, asset-backed securities, futures, options, foreign exchange, derivatives, and others. Because a salesperson works largely on commission, there are major bucks to be made, especially with some of the high-volume accounts.

Sales professionals are typically responsible for the following:

- Developing strong relationships with institutional investors

- Meeting with economic and equity research departments to discuss economic and industry trends and their impact on the markets

- Working with the investment banking department to market new debt and equity issues

- Assisting and advising clients in developing and executing investment strategies

- Watching company/industry/economic/political news and market activity, and advising clients about the likely impact on their portfolios

- Attending company presentations and research conferences, typically with clients

- Arranging meetings between clients, research analysts, and company management

Trading

Traders are responsible for taking positions in the market through purchases and sales of equities (stocks), debt (bonds), and other securities. Trading functions are typically divided by the product lines offered by the investment bank. It's not a job for the meek, timid, or easily offended. During market hours, all trading floors are loud, high-energy environments. Traders must juggle several phone lines, scan computer screens flashing headlines and quotes, and respond to orders from salespeople—all while executing trades with precision timing. The firm's capital is on the line, and every second can be worth millions.

Traders are typically responsible for the following:

- Developing a solid knowledge of market, company, and industry information (An insider says, "A good trader is constantly on top of what's going on.")

- Evaluating market activity and supply/demand indications from salespeople and clients

- "Making markets"—maintain a position in a stock the firm has underwritten, quote bid and ask prices, and buy and sell at those prices

- Advising salespeople, clients, and research analysts on market activity and pricing for different stock and equity issues

- Putting major trades together by negotiating with salespeople/clients and other dealers

- Performing valuation analysis of derivatives, convertibles, or baskets of stocks

- Managing the firm's investment risk

MAKING IT

Typical Career Paths

One typical path for a salesperson or trader goes like this: He or she gets a foot in the door on Wall Street by getting a position as an assistant on a trading or sales desk—for instance, on a foreign-equities desk, or corporate fixed-income desk. (Those who have done internships in the field during college will have the best shot at these positions.) Through hard work and experience, the assistant works his or her way up to an analyst position on that desk. If the assistant doesn't make it to analyst, he or she returns to school to get an MBA and then gets a job at his or her old bank or another bank as a sales or trading associate.

Another typical path: The would-be trader or salesperson starts his or her career in another field, and then goes back to school to get an MBA. While in B-school, he or she decides to pursue a career in sales or trading, takes courses targeted at that career, gets an internship in the field between the first and second years of B-school, and then gets a full-time associate position in sales or trading after graduation.

What It Takes

Sales jobs and trading jobs have many overlapping skill requirements, such as verbal communication skills, sales skills, and a facility for numbers. But the people who do well in each

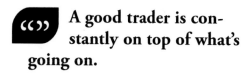 **A good trader is constantly on top of what's going on.**

area are not identical. For example, salespeople have to be good at building relationships with a variety of personality types, whereas traders only have to be good at building relationships with other traders. Salespeople have to be good at giving presentations, whereas traders have to be good at making snap decisions based on constantly changing information. Sales jobs typically require a lot more travel than do trading jobs. People in both careers have to be aggressive self-starters.

Salespeople and traders both need to be able to deal with a lot of stress. For instance, because salespeople are essentially account managers, they're the ones who have to take the heat from a client who is irate that a particular stock in his or her portfolio is falling. It's not easy keeping all of the people happy all of the time, especially in a down market. Meanwhile, on the bank's trading floor, the action never stops while the market is in session. (In case you haven't seen a trading floor, it looks something like NASA's Mission Control, only instead of dozens of sleepy-looking engineers, the room is dominated by clean-cut twenty-somethings, most of whom have their sleeves rolled up and are often talking on several phones at once.) While the market is open, traders are pretty much tied to their spot on the desk, which is an inch away from the next trader's and jam-packed with multiple computer screens. Amidst all that hubbub and all those demands for one's attention, traders get to stress over whether their investment decisions will pay off.

People in both of these careers will have to take exams to become licensed in their area of specialty. For example, most salespeople have to pass the Series 7 exam.

Unlike other investment banking careers, it's not always necessary to get a graduate degree to advance up the ladder in sales or trading.

Note that you're most likely to get your career in sales or trading started if you have great grades from an Ivy League or similarly prestigious school. (And, the old-boy network is alive and well on Wall Street.) This is not to say that getting one of these careers will be impossible if you don't—just that it'll be even more difficult than it is for the Ivy League kids with great grades, many of whom will be rejected for entry-level jobs in these careers themselves.

The Odds: Fair

As with other investment banking careers, perhaps the hardest part of this career path is getting your foot in the door in the first place. Investment banks, especially the top-tier banks like Goldman Sachs, Lehman Brothers, Citigroup, Morgan Stanley, Merrill Lynch, Bear Stearns, and Credit Suisse First Boston, which have the most jobs for people in these fields, are notoriously picky when it comes to hiring. Once you're in, if you perform (i.e., if you make your bank money), you'll move up—and you'll get paid handsomely.

People who leave these fields may find themselves well-suited for sales jobs in other industries, or, if they're more comfortable with a calmer atmosphere than is typical at a sales or trading desk, in research analyst positions either on the sell side (within an investment bank) or on the buy side (at a hedge fund or mutual fund, e.g.).

ADDITIONAL RESOURCES

Beat the Street series of investment banking interview guides (WetFeet Insider Guides, available from www.WetFeet.com)

Careers in Investment Banking (WetFeet Insider Guide, available from www.WetFeet.com)

Investment Dealers' Digest (www.iddmagazine.com)

Investopedia.com

Killer Investment Banking Resumes! (WetFeet Insider Guide, available from www.WetFeet.com)

PROFILE

John Meriwether, Trader

If his current life is any indication, in his previous life John Meriwether must have been a cat. After all, after coming from humble beginnings, he's already in his third life as a Wall Street pro. First, he was a star trader at Salomon Brothers, one of the featured players in *Liar's Poker*, the bestselling expose of 1980s Wall Street culture by Michael Lewis. (In the book, he's alleged to have made a $10 million bet with Salomon CEO John Gutfreund—on a single poker hand.) He resigned that position in 1991, though, during a scandal over improper Treasury-auction bids submitted by his group at Salomon.

Within a year, though, Meriwether was back on the scene, this time as the head of Long-Term Capital Management (LTCM), a hedge fund with $1 billion in capital supplied by Merrill Lynch. The team at LTCM thought they'd found a surefire way to beat the market—a mathematically foolproof means of doing arbitrage investments, which try to take advantage of variations in price between similar investments—and proceeded to make hugely leveraged investments using their system. Unfortunately, in 1998, the market turned against them, and LTCM collapsed. Its almost $100 billion in debt nearly brought down the global economy around it, but the firm was bailed out by other Wall Street firms.

Lo and behold, Meriwether, who worked as a golf caddy as a young man, went to business school at the University of Chicago, and started working at Salomon Brothers in 1974, now has another hedge fund. JWM Partners is a leveraged arbitrage fund using a similar strategy to the one used by LTCM. It's also proof that Meriwether has lived to trade another day.

Law Firm Partner

WHAT YOU CAN MAKE

Equity partners at big law firms can make more than $1 million per year in profit payouts, in addition to their already pretty snazzy salaries, depending on how their firms perform during the year.

JOB DESCRIPTION

In broad terms, lawyers apply their interpretation of the law (the codified rules of their society) to advise their employer or client on completing transactions in compliance with the law or resolving disputes based on current understanding of the law.

At its most basic level, a lawyer's role is that of an advocate and adviser. Attorneys use specialized knowledge to research and interpret the intent of the law and apply it to whatever circumstances their clients face.

The legal profession can be divided into two major categories: litigation and transactions. Litigation, which concerns both civil and criminal law, is the process of arguing a dispute between two parties. Transactions relate to business and personal matters that usually do not require courtroom argumentation. For example, a lawyer may counsel a client in preparing a will, contract, or lease; help secure venture capital for a new company; or prepare a patent for a new technology. Litigation and transactions have specializations of their own, such as tax, antitrust, bankruptcy, labor, real estate, insurance, international trade, environmental regulation, and mergers and acquisitions—to name just a few. Lawyers can also specialize in specific industries such as health care, high tech, life sciences, entertainment, or even nonprofits.

Depending on the type of law they practice, lawyers will spend their time on paper-work; researching, preparing for, or participating in trials; and advising clients. They spend hours in law libraries and with online databases researching legal precedents. They prepare contracts, briefs, and other documents, assembling boilerplate paragraphs or writing text from scratch.

They plan and conduct depositions (interviews with witnesses), which in complicated cases can generate thousands of pages of testimony—all of which have to be read, ana-lyzed, and refined into usable information. They may present their evidence—the infor-mation they've gathered about a case and about the laws relevant to a case—in a court of law, arguing before a judge or jury. Alternatively, they may present their research findings to clients, advising them on business or other issues.

Law firm partners typically handle their firms' biggest most important cases and clients. They also manage associates who are helping them with their cases, as well as managing more-seasoned associates who are overseeing their own cases or clients. Partners may also sit on committees overseeing the finances of the firm, or personnel decisions, or other operational or administrative matters. Finally, a big part of the typical partner's responsibilities is maintaining existing client relationships and relationships with poten-tial clients, in order to win new business for the firm.

MAKING IT

Typical Career Paths

Would-be law firm partners prepare for their careers by going to law school. The better the school, and the better their grades, the better their opportunities will be after grad-uation. (Notable extracurriculars, such as working on the Law Review, also help when it comes time to get a job.) Most law students do summer internships at law firms.

After graduation, most would-be firm partners go to work for law firms, though some will take a temporary detour and do a clerkship with a judge.

To practice law, of course, would-be lawyers next need to pass their state's bar exam; this can involve a months of intense study. Often, firms will hire new law-school graduates to full-time jobs even before they take the bar, with the understanding that, if they don't pass after taking the exam once or twice, they won't continue with the firm.

After that comes a long stretch as an associate. At first, this means assisting partners and more-seasoned associates by doing research for the cases they're overseeing. As time passes, more-experienced associates will usually start to handle their own cases, which depending on the kind of law they're practicing can mean making arguments in court. Finally, after 6 to 10 years, the associate is either offered a partnership position or asked to leave the firm.

What It Takes

In terms of formal requirements, lawyers need to be licensed in the state where they practice. This, of course, means passing the dreaded state bar exam. (While technically you don't need to have gone to law school to practice law, for all practical purposes law school is also a formal requirement for would-be law firm partners.)

Beyond the formal requirements, working as a lawyer requires excellent and persuasive oral and written communication skills (English majors: Here's a chance to prove grandpa wrong and use your degree for something useful and lucrative!) as you'll be required to interpret complicated, and sometimes ambiguous, laws in such a way that backs up your clients, while maintaining the integrity of the legal system (at least ideally). Lawyers must be detail-oriented, natural negotiators who enjoy research. And they must also have a high tolerance for tedium—there can be a lot of paperwork involved. As one insider says, "A lot of lawyerly tasks are incredibly tedious—6,000 pages of scientific reports on groundwater pollution from aluminum manufacturing is not what I'd call engaging literature."

The Odds: Fair

If you really want to become a law firm partner, the chances are fair that you'll succeed. Whether you'll be able to become a super-high-income partner at a major firm is a different story, though. The competition to get associate positions at the major firms is intense—and even if you do manage to get your foot in the door, there's a chance you won't make partner. The key to making it to the top ranks of your firm is total dedication to that pursuit. If you're hired by a top firm, you'll know you've got the smarts to succeed. Now all you need to do to make partner is put in the hours and make building business for the firm your top priority in life. It may wreak havoc on your personal life—what little personal life you'll have—but this is almost certainly the kind of attitude you'll need to make it to the top.

> **A lot of lawyerly tasks are incredibly tedious—6,000 pages of scientific reports on groundwater pollution from aluminum manufacturing is not what I'd call engaging literature.**

Luckily, the skills you learn in law school and in the workplace can take you a long way in your career, even if you don't want to work in a firm for the rest of your life. In fact, a legal background is great experience for almost any industry or profession. You'll find lawyers in politics, finance, sports, and all kinds of other industries, in careers ranging from banking to business development to film and TV production. Of course, lawyers can also find jobs as in-house attorneys at companies in industry, or they can hang out their own shingle and become a solo practitioner. Finally, many lawyers also end up teaching law.

ADDITIONAL RESOURCES

American Bar Association (www.abanet.org)

FindLaw (www.findlaw.com)

Hieros Gamos (www.hg.org)

Law.com

WetFeet's Law Career Profile (www.wetfeet.com/asp/careerprofiles_track.
asp?careerpk=21)

PROFILE

Robert S. Bennett, Law Firm Partner

Bob Bennett is a partner at Skadden, Arps, Slate, Meagher & Flom—one of the biggest, most powerful law firms in the world—where he heads up the firm's global enforcement group, as well as the firm's D.C. criminal and civil litigation practice. Among other responsibilities, Bennett advises and represents corporations, directors, and officers in civil, criminal, and securities-regulation disputes.

Bennett has had a long career in law, much of it in the public eye. He represented Bill Clinton in the Paula Jones sexual harassment case. He represented Enron. He was Special Counsel to the Senate's Select Committee on Ethics for a number of investigations. And he acted as legal consultant to the Senate Foreign Relations Committee when President Ronald Reagan appointed Alexander Haig as Secretary of State, back in the 1980s. Other Bennett clients have included Marge Schott, owner of the Cincinnati Reds baseball franchise, and Caspar Weinberger, former Secretary of Defense under Ronald Reagan.

Bennett, who was an amateur boxer in his younger days, was born in Brooklyn, into a tumultuous family life; his mother married five times. (His little brother Bill was Secretary of Education under Reagan and the Bush drug czar.) After graduating from Harvard Law School, he clerked for a federal judge in Washington, D.C., before becoming a federal prosecutor. After a stint at a big law firm, he helped start a small firm, which was later acquired by Skadden, Arps.

Literary, Sports, or Talent Agent

WHAT YOU CAN MAKE

Say you represent Kobe Bryant. Say he's paying you 5 percent of his income for your agenting services. Now, figure Bryant is making $26 million this year—that means you're making $1.3 million. And Kobe's just one of your clients! In other words, if you can land the right clients, being an agent can be a very lucrative profession.

JOB DESCRIPTION

An agent is a business representative of people with a talent or talents that others may be willing to pay money to employ. Agents find business opportunities for their clients and negotiate compensation for them when they find work for their clients. Agents make money by taking a percentage of what their clients make.

There are a variety of types of agents. The most common (and most lucrative) types are literary agents (who represent books and authors), talent agents (who represent actors, musicians, directors, and screenwriters), and sports agents (who represent professional athletes). In some agent-client relationships, the agent's only job is to negotiate contracts for the client. In other agent-client relationships, the agent plays a much bigger role, in essence guiding the client through his or her career, doing things like coaching the client, hiring expert help for the client, creating promotional materials for the client, and so on.

Literary agents look for talented authors and compelling books to represent. They read through book manuscripts and proposals that are submitted to them by hopeful writers, looking for people and projects they think might be attractive to publishers. When they find something they like, they sign the author to a contract that makes the agent that author's exclusive agent for a given period. They then submit their client's work to publishers; when a publisher is interested in buying the client's work, the agent negotiates the deal. Literary agents also find writing assignments for their clients, such as magazine-article assignments.

Talent agents are much like literary agents, only they represent actors, musicians, and TV, film, and theater writers and directors. Talent agents send actors they represent to TV, film, or theater auditions. They send screenplays and new TV-show proposals to studios and production companies. They're constantly on the lookout for new talent to represent, whether that means signing up-and-coming talent or poaching already-successful clients from rival agents.

Sports agents have the same basic responsibilities for their athlete clients; they talk to sports teams to try to drum up interest in their clients, and negotiate their clients' contracts. They may also be involved in getting their clients commercial endorsement work. As sports agent Kenneth Chase says, "You'd be amazed how many businesses want to be identified with a professional athlete. I mean it's not just Michael Jordan and Nike—these million-dollar endorsements—there's a whole range of situations. You're opening a new restaurant or Footlocker? You get a football player to show up, that's great. Instant credibility. Or a regional advertising campaign. There's so many opportunities." (*Gig*, Crown Publishers, 2000)

Agents usually differ from managers in that they're focused on finding their clients work, and negotiating their work contracts. Managers are typically involved in managing a wide range of their clients' business affairs, which can mean anything from scheduling performances to helping their clients make investment decisions and keeping track of their clients' financial statements.

Most agents spend a significant amount of their time networking with others in their business. For instance, it's part of the sports agent's job to know what various teams' personnel needs are, so that he or she can offer a given team a particular client's services if there's a match between that team's needs and the client's abilities. And it's part of the talent agent's job to know what scripts the different production companies around town are developing, so that the agent can be sure to send clients to all the auditions that make sense for them.

MAKING IT

Typical Career Paths

Many Hollywood agents start their careers working for a movie or TV studio or production company. At the big Hollywood talent agencies, new agent-track hires often begin in the mailroom, from which vantage point they learn the business.

Literary agents often begin their careers working as junior editors at publishing companies before going to work for their first literary agency.

Many would-be agents find great value in going to law school. Would-be talent and literary agents usually find it necessary to move to L.A. or New York, where the greatest concentration of people and companies (and therefore business opportunities) in their industries are found. There, they go to work for agencies, where they usually learn their craft in a sink-or-swim environment.

What It Takes

There are no educational requirements for many agents. Most do have at least a BA, though, and many agents find that an MBA or JD gives them advantages in doing their jobs, especially when it comes to negotiating contracts and making other business decisions.

Many agents have to get licensed in order to represent particular kinds of clients. Agents for Hollywood TV and film actors, for instance, are usually licensed by the Screen Actors Guild. And sports agents are often licensed to represent the kind of athletes they represent; for instance, football players' agents are usually licensed by the National Football League Players Association.

Beyond the educational and formal requirements, successful agents are typically very passionate about the industry they're part of. Hollywood agents typically have a deep appreciation of the art and craft of making movies and TV shows, for instance. Literary agents love books. And sports agents? Right: They love sports. As an insider puts it, "There's something special about being able to work in a job where you love the product."

Good agents are also creative (as in, able to find ways to make negotiations that seem doomed to fall apart work to satisfaction of both the client and the client's would-be employer). They're hardworking self-starters; if they don't make the phone calls and get their clients work, after all, they won't make any money. They're good at networking. They have a strong attention to detail. They are able to strategize, both to help their clients plan their careers, and to plan their own careers. They understand the needs of the would-be purchasers of their clients' products or services—whether that means sports teams, Hollywood production companies, or publishing companies. They are good communicators who can sell their clients' would-be employers on why their clients are so very right for the jobs in question. They are leaders who are able to motivate staff to provide the best possible service for clients and able to motivate clients when they're going through periods in which they're getting little work. And they're aggressive; aggressiveness is one of the big prerequisites for achieving big-time success as an agent. The successful agent knows he's not really being annoying when he calls someone for the 15th time to tout one of his clients; rather, he's making sure the recipient of his call is fully aware of the business opportunities that will open before him if he hires the agent's client.

The Odds: Poor

While there are tens of thousands of agents of different kinds in the United States, the big-money agents form a small, very exclusive club. Even if you fail to become a millionaire as an agent, there's a decent chance you'll make a pretty good living through your work.

ADDITIONAL RESOURCES

Association of Talent Agents (www.agentassociation.com)

Careers in Entertainment and Sports (WetFeet Insider Guide, available from www.WetFeet.com)

iSeek's Sports Agents and Business Managers page (www.iseek.org/sv/13000. jsp?id=100228)

PROFILE

Dave Wirtschafter, Talent Agent

In an industry known as being full of glad-handers and schmoozers, Dave Wirtschafter is known for being relatively bloodless, for being a technocrat of sorts. He's an agent who prefers staying at home reading scripts to going out and patting colleagues' shoulders and giving actresses air-kisses at Hollywood cocktail parties. But he's a major success, thanks to the long hours he puts in on the job (most nights, he reads scripts for 3 hours, falls asleep at 10:30, and then wakes up in the wee hours of the morning to read more scripts and plan what he'll do when he gets to the office) and to his ability to negotiate innovative, lucrative contracts for his clients.

Wirtshafter, who grew up in San Pedro, California, just south of Los Angeles, is the president of the William Morris Agency, a storied Hollywood agency. He began his career while he was in law school at the University of Southern California, taking a job in the mailroom at Creative Artists Agency, another big agency. While there, he read the script for the then-unmade movie *Hoosiers* and thought that Gene Hackman would make a perfect fit for the lead role. He gave the script to a friend who worked with Hackman's agent, and Hackman ended up being cast in the role. Wirtschafter was promoted to a business affairs position, then went to work at another agency, International Creative Management, in 1986. In 1999, when Jim Wiatt, the president of I.C.M., was hired away by William Morris, Wirtschafter followed him.

Wirtschafter's client list includes directors and writers Ridley Scott, Gus Van Sant, the Wachowski brothers (of *Matrix* fame), and Spike Lee, and actors and musicians Halle Berry, Chris Tucker, and Alicia Keys; he has some 40 clients in total.

Professional Athlete

WHAT YOU CAN MAKE

We all know that professional athletes—at least male athletes, in big-money professional sports—can make mountains of money. But just how high are those mountains? The following list, of the 25 best-paid athletes in 2004, should give you a clearer picture:

Athlete	Sport	Compensation ($M)
Tiger Woods	Golf	80.3
Michael Schumacher	Auto racing	80.0
Peyton Manning	Football	42.0
Michael Jordan	Basketball (retired)	35.0
Shaquille O'Neal	Basketball	31.9
Kevin Garnett	Basketball	29.7
Andre Agassi	Tennis	28.2
David Beckham	Soccer	28.0
Alex Rodriguez	Baseball	26.2
Kobe Bryant	Basketball	26.1
Grant Hill	Basketball	25.9
Derek Jeter	Baseball	23.2
Barry Bonds	Baseball	22.7
Manny Ramirez	Baseball	22.1
Oscar de la Hoya	Boxing	22.0
LeBron James	Basketball	21.1
Vince Carter	Basketball	20.2
Dale Earnhardt Jr.	Auto racing	20.1
Arnold Palmer	Golf	20.0
Phil Mickelson	Golf	19.8

Athlete	Sport	2004 Compensation ($M)
Allen Iverson	Basketball	19.7
Champ Bailey	Football	19.6
Jeff Gordon	Auto racing	19.3
Lance Armstrong	Cycling	19.2
Tracy McGrady	Basketball	19.0

Sources: Forbes.com; WetFeet analysis.

JOB DESCRIPTION

The job description varies from sport to sport (and even athlete to athlete). All professional athletes spend a lot of time training, though. This can involve everything from off-season weight training to help an athlete become stronger and more durable to, famously in the case of ex-NFL player Herschel Walker, learning to dance ballet (Walker believed dancing improved his balance and coordination). It also involves practice time—the daily practices NFL players participate in between each successive Sunday during the football season, or the month of spring training in Arizona or Florida before the regular season starts for Major League Baseball players.

Of course, the core of most professional athletes' jobs is to compete, whether that means playing in a regular-season or playoff NBA game, driving in a NASCAR auto race, or dropping into the vert ramp at the X-Games.

Beyond training for and actually participating in their sport, many athletes have to make a significant number of public appearances in their community or across the country (think of the many public-service TV ads you've seen over the years, showing hulking professional athletes in a classroom teaching cute li'l tykes to read). Some also spend time being photographed or recorded for TV, print, or radio commercials. Finally, professional sports invariably involves quite a bit of travel.

MAKING IT

Typical Career Paths

Typically, professional athletes begin playing their sport of choice at an early age. They excel early on and end up playing on all-star teams and in high-level summer leagues and going to cream-of-the-crop summer camps for their sports. Depending on their sport, they may be observed by college or professional scouts and coaches. The athlete's job at this point is primarily to keep improving at his or her sport; some are physically gifted enough to progress from this stage to the pros, but for the most part, at this point, to fulfill their potential and attain real success in their sport, athletes need to work to become stronger, faster, and more skilled. Good coaching can really make the difference for athletes at this stage, and smart young athletes will seek out good coaching wherever and whenever they can find it.

Eventually, the best of the best in each sport end up playing professionally. This can happen in a variety of ways. Some athletes, particularly in team sports, are drafted by professional teams. Others make it to the pros by performing well at team tryouts, which can be open to all comers or invitation-only. Other athletes in individual sports, such as auto racing or surfing, make it to the top levels of the pros by excelling at increasingly difficult levels of competition—by driving less-powerful cars on a more regional racing circuit, for instance, before breaking through and making it onto the NASCAR circuit.

As should be obvious by now, the typical career path for a professional athlete varies depending on the sport. Baseball players can be drafted right out of high school, for instance, though they'll typically spend years in the minor leagues before they get the chance to be one of the lucky few in the majors. Still, many baseball players choose to take scholarships to play in college before entering the baseball draft.

Basketball players are more likely to go to college than baseball players, though that's been changing over the past decade or so. A number of very successful NBA players, such as Kobe Bryant, Jermaine O'Neal, Kevin Garnett, and LeBron James, were drafted right out of high school. And those who do go to college are more and more likely to leave college and enter the draft after just a year or 2 following high school. Currently, the NBA is debating whether to require high school athletes to go to college for at least a short while before they can turn pro.

Football players are still pretty much required to go to college. The legality of that requirement is currently up for debate, but even if it is established that players can legally be drafted before they've played 4 years in college, the physical and mental demands of the NFL make it extremely likely that most players will indeed play their entire college career before pro teams will consider drafting them.

Finally, hockey players are typically drafted at a young age, then play minor league hockey before they develop enough to merit playing time in the NHL.

What It Takes

The most obvious component here is physical talent. Do you have a 36-inch vertical jump? Can you bench-press 300 pounds? Can you sprint 40 yards in under 4.6 seconds? Do your muscles recover quickly from stress? Do you have lightning-fast reflexes, or way-above-average hand-eye coordination? There are certain raw skills that predispose individuals to succeed in any given sport.

Those raw skills are rarely enough to get athletes to the pros in their sport, though, much less to result in sustained success and a chance at reaching the all-star level among pro athletes. To soar that high, athletes need to possess a number of attributes, including a strong competitive drive, an ability to stay focused, and the drive to work hard to continue to improve. Michael Jordan, for instance, was renowned for working hard to gain new basketball skills every off-season, and for maintaining his strength by supplementing in-season games and practices with private weight-lifting sessions—even after he'd earned the reputation of being the greatest basketball player ever. In *Gig*, pro hockey player Shawn McEachern stresses the nonphysical aspects of being a professional athlete: "It's very mental. I mean, everybody playing pro hockey is a pretty good player. Everybody's got good skills. . . . It's a long season. It wears you down. . . . But you still have to concentrate. You gotta be able to just shake it off and focus."

Other skills that come in handy for professional athletes include a willingness to be coached; flexibility, or an ability to analyze any given situation and understand how one's particular skills and talent should be used to perform as well as possible in that situation; and an ability to tune out distractions and focus on the situation at hand. (For example, have you ever admired how some basketball players can make last-second free throws despite intense heckling from the opposing team's fans? That's what we're talking about.)

Finally, athletes who want to supplement their income via commercials and product endorsements are well advised to develop the friendly side of their personalities, and avoid getting involved with unsavory characters or in legally or ethically questionable activities. (Of course, some would argue the opposite—that "street cred" can go a long way to giving an athlete public notoriety—but in the long run, the bad-boy athletes typically don't make as much as media-friendly athletes, especially when it comes to product endorsements.)

The Odds: Poor

Seemingly every little boy wants to grow up to be a professional baseball player, or football player, or what have you. Very, very few of them make it. Think about it: There are only spots for a few hundred professional athletes in each of the major sports leagues. Only the very best make it to the pro level. Some of those don't even make it, thanks to injuries or bad luck. For the rest of us, the dream of playing pro sports will always be just that—a dream.

Which is why it's important for athletes who aspire to go pro to prepare to do something other than play their sport for a living. There aren't many paying fields to which you'll be able to directly transfer the skills and knowledge you gained playing your sport. If you don't make it to the pros, you might be able to coach, or teach physical education, with minimal additional training. If you think you might be interested in doing something else, start preparing now for the possibility that you don't make the pros.

ADDITIONAL RESOURCES

Bureau of Labor Statistics' Athletes, Coaches, Umpires, and Related Workers page (stats.bls.gov/oco/ocos251.htm)

"A Career in Professional Athletics" (NCAA booklet, download PDF from www.ncaa.org/library/general/career_in_pro_athletics/2004-05/2004-05_career_pro_athletics.pdf)

iSeek's Professional Athletes page (www.iseek.org/sv/13000.jsp?id=100425)

PROFILE

Dwayne Wade, Professional Basketball Player

Dwayne "Flash" Wade plays guard for the Miami Heat of the National Basketball Association. He was drafted fifth overall by the Heat in 2003; he played well in his rookie season, making the All-NBA Rookie First Team, but was often overshadowed by LeBron James and Carmelo Anthony, media darlings who were selected #1 and #2 in the 2003 draft. Wade started getting more attention during the 2004 playoffs and then was named to the 2004 U.S. Olympic basketball team. Now, at the end of his sophomore season in the NBA, during which he also played in the 2004 All-Star Game, he is thought to be on the verge of superstardom.

An explosive, slashing player, Wade attended college at Marquette University, which he helped make the Final Four in the 2003 NCAA Basketball Tournament. He left before his senior season to enter the NBA draft. At Marquette, Wade majored in broadcasting, because he wants to work in the field when his playing career in over.

Broadcasting can wait, though, at least for a little while. Wade now counts Shaquille O'Neal among his teammates, which means the Heat will probably contend for the NBA championship for at least the next couple of years. Wade may tithe part of his substantial income to his hometown church, but it's not like he isn't enjoying having money; he counts buying shoes among his interests, despite the challenges having size-15 feet must pose when it comes time to practice his hobby.

Wade earned a salary of some $2.8 million for the 2004–05 season, but after making the all-star team and developing into a budding superstar, he stands to make much more than that per season once his current contract ends.

Real Estate Developer or Investor

WHAT YOU CAN MAKE

How much can you make as a real estate developer? A lot. Consider Donald Trump. In 2004, he earned more than $6 million in total compensation from Trump Hotels & Casinos—and that company represents just a small piece of this guy's myriad real estate interests. His organization owns everything from prime New York real estate like Trump Tower, the Plaza Hotel, and the land beneath the Javits Convention Center to golf courses in New York, Florida, and California. Despite what you'll occasionally read about the ill health of some of his investments, Trump is doing just fine. And that's not even considering his paycheck for *The Apprentice*.

JOB DESCRIPTION

Developers are responsible for taking a property idea and making it a reality. This is a complex process involving architects, engineers, zoning officials, builders, lenders, and prospective tenants. Development is not always the gravy train some make it out to be. In the early 1990s, when real estate prices crashed, construction dried up and a lot of commercial office space was left vacant. Deprived of rents, a lot of developers had to scramble for survival. Many ventured into other areas of real estate. Today, many of the largest real estate developers are also property owners and managers.

Commercial developers perform or coordinate land acquisition and assembly, negotiation, government relationships, finance, design, and construction of buildings as well as leasing and sales for commercial, industrial, or residential properties. Because of the cost, scope, and time involved in commercial developments, a single firm rarely performs all functions; instead, developers rely on relationships with firms in allied industries.

Residential developers perform many of the same tasks as their commercial counterparts, but their work is more limited in scope by their end products, which tend to be single-family homes and low-density housing. Like commercial developers, residential developers are involved in coordinating financing, architectural services, and construction management. In an effort to pull in a larger share of the home-buyer's wallet, companies have been moving downstream, offering a whole suite of products including mortgage origination, title services, broadband and phone services, as well as premium options such as kitchen islands and high-end appliances.

NOT FOR WALLFLOWERS

"Real estate is by all measures a people business," says an insider. Industry professionals work in the same markets for many years and cultivate deep relationships that transcend business.

MAKING IT

Typical Career Paths

Many developers get their start as development company project managers. Project managers oversee the full life cycle of the development process from site selection to construction. A project manager might perform due diligence with respect to land acquisitions, negotiate with government agencies, secure the proper permits for development, prepare and manage project budgets, and manage contractors through the construction process. Project managers often arrive at their positions after working in construction management or architecture.

What It Takes

If you have the right skills and are undaunted by the vicissitudes of the industry, real estate can afford a phenomenally challenging and rewarding career.

Any kind of investing in real estate requires a thorough understanding of how to analyze the value of a property and navigate the maze of land-use regulations, zoning laws, environmental impact reports, financing realities, and other barriers to buying and developing a property. The people who develop, market, and manage REITs and other real estate investments are financial types, often MBAs, who are charged with evaluating and arranging for the purchase of properties.

 PUTTING DOWN ROOTS

Real estate requires an intimate knowledge of idiosyncratic geographic markets that takes many years to master; even Donald Trump only operates in Manhattan and Atlantic City.

"You cannot switch markets without starting over to some degree," says one insider. If you like being tied down to a single community, real estate should work for you; if you've got wanderlust, beware.

People skills are paramount in real estate. Everyone, from brokers to investment fund partners, relies on the relationships they forge throughout their careers to find clients and understand the subtleties and caprices of the market. Professional real estate investors need a well-honed financial and analytical tool kit to evaluate the investment potential of properties as well as keen sales and marketing instincts to sell not only their developments, but also their funds to investors. Project management skills are as critical to the tasks of ongoing asset and property management as they are to coordinating large-scale deals. Finally, people who endure in the industry have the fortitude to see themselves through the famine of down markets.

Developers should have a strong understanding of business in general and the real estate industry in particular. A college degree with course work in architecture, labor management, business, law, economics, and engineering is helpful, if not necessary. Most developers have previous real estate experience, but they can also enter the field as assistants working for development firms.

The Odds: Fair

The growing population, and wealth, of the United States translates to continued long-term growth in both commercial and residential markets nationwide, which translates to growing numbers of opportunities for real estate developers.

In terms of what other kinds of opportunities working in real estate development can lead to, the development sector has a reputation as being a good training ground for real estate investment and asset management positions.

ADDITIONAL RESOURCES

Careers in Real Estate (WetFeet Insider Guide, available from www.WetFeet.com)

Development magazine (www.naiop.org/developmentmag/index.cfm)

National Real Estate Investor magazine (www.nreionline.com)

Real Estate Research at the Haas Business School (groups.haas.berkeley.edu/realestate/Research/researchinfo.asp)

PROFILE

Donald Trump, Real Estate Developer

Donald Trump (a.k.a. The Donald) was born in New York City in 1946. He grew up rich, thanks to the success of his father, Fred, who was also a real estate developer. Apparently, The Donald was not The Achiever as a kid; his parents sent him to military school when he was 13 in an effort to get him on the right track. It must have worked, since Trump ended up going to Fordham and then transferring to the University of Pennsylvania, where he got his bachelor's in 1968.

Trump arrived on the national stage in the 1980s, when he used a series of loans requiring little in the way of collateral to build an impressive portfolio of real estate. He stamped his name on all his properties (e.g., Trump Tower on 5th Avenue in New York and the Trump Taj Mahal hotel and casino in Atlantic City), married an exotic Czech beauty (Ivana), and ended up a staple in the New York gossip pages—and very, very rich.

Trump's business life has seen its share of ups and downs, just like his personal life. He's been married three times (most recently, in 2004, he married Melania Knauss). And his major business ventures have twice declared bankruptcy; The Trump Organization restructured its debt in 1990, and in 2004 Trump Hotels & Casino Resorts declared Chapter 11 bankruptcy. Still, The Donald's doing just fine, thank you. His real estate holdings include everything from golf courses in Florida and California to office and apartment towers in New York, with future developments including hotels and condos in Florida and Arizona. Apparently, being your own boss means never having to listen to anyone else says the words, "You're fired!"

Trump reportedly earned some $7 million in 2004.

Rock, Hip-Hop, or Pop Star

WHAT YOU CAN MAKE

Most musical acts don't make anywhere near what you'd think they do, even if they do know how to party like, well, rock stars. But for those at the top of the music heap, the financial rewards can be ample. As in, $25 million per year in income for Aerosmith. Or about $40 million per year for Madonna and Britney Spears. Or as much as $70 million per year if you're in the same class as U2.

JOB DESCRIPTION

You've probably seen the *Making the Album* and *Behind the Music* shows on music-oriented cable TV stations, and you may think you have a pretty good idea of what being a rock, pop, or hip-hop star involves. What you may not realize, though, is that much of what you see on those programs is not necessarily part of the story for most musical acts. The spiral into drug and alcohol abuse . . . the knock-down, drag-out arguments in the recording studio . . . the tragic loss of the original bass player in the bus accident . . . the arrest for involvement in the shooting outside the nightclub. . . . None of these things is part of the formal job description for rock, pop, and hip-hop stars.

Rock, pop, and hip-hop stars' main job is to record and perform music. Musicians who write their own music also spend time writing new material to record and perform. Recording involves spending time in recording studios, performing, and mixing music until it's ready to release to the public. Performing usually involves touring from venue to venue, giving concerts. It can also involve appearing on TV and radio programs, promoting the artist's current CD or concert tour by performing one or more songs live.

Highly successful musical acts also typically spend a lot of time dealing with the press, doing interviews and being approached by journalists and photographers at awards presentations and other industry events.

MAKING IT

Typical Career Paths

Most musicians who make it big are not overnight successes, even if you've never heard of them before. Most have long histories of playing in a variety of musical groups, of recording and performing on a local or regional level for years before attaining break-out success. Consider rapper 50 Cent. He was known regionally in the New York area for a number of years, thanks to his local performances and the appearance of his songs on underground mix tapes, before Eminem discovered him and signed him to his record label.

Success for aspiring pop, rock, and hip-hop stars typically comes when a particular song or album recorded by the artist sells massively and becomes a mainstay in popular culture. But that's only the first step in becoming a true star. Unless you want to end up mentioned on *Where Are They Now?* VH1 shows about one-hit wonders, you'll need to keep pumping out music that sells.

What It Takes

There are no formal requirements for becoming a rock, pop, or hip-hop star. The main requirement is talent—having a voice that is beautiful or otherwise compelling, and an ability to play music that people want to hear. As a result, many musicians and singers commit significant time to formal studies of their craft.

To become a big-time star, it's usually necessary to have good looks, charisma, or both. Think about it: There are probably thousands of singers as good as Shania Twain out there, but without her looks (and, therefore, her marketability). And your band will never, ever be as big as U2 or the Rolling Stones if your singer doesn't have the innate ability of Bono or Mick Jagger to mesmerize an audience.

It's also necessary to be persistent. Many musical acts languish in obscurity for years or even decades before breaking out.

The Odds: Poor

Most pop, rock, and hip-hop artists never attain success beyond the local or regional level. Most would-be music stars look forward eagerly to the day they get signed by a major record label—but that achievement does not guarantee success. The vast majority of pop, rock, and hip-hop recordings—even among those released by major record labels—achieve only modest sales. This can be due to the fact that the musical act does not strike the public's fancy or because the record label does not put major marketing dollars behind an act's recording.

ADDITIONAL RESOURCES

Berklee College of Music's Music Careers page (www.berklee.edu/careers/default.html)

Music Biz Academy.com's Career Planning page (www.musicbizacademy.com/knab/articles/careerplanning.htm)

SoloPerformer's Music Careers page (www.soloperformer.com/careers)

PROFILE

Björk, Singer/Songwriter

Björk's first big musical success came when she was a member of the Sugarcubes, the angular-pop-rock band that was the first internationally famous Icelandic rock act. The Sugarcubes burst on the global scene with the release of the band's first album, *Life's Too Good*, in 1988; the band would dissolve only 4 years later, in 1992, amidst tension between Björk and the male singer in the band. Already, when she was in the Sugarcubes, the pixie-ish Björk was beginning to achieve some international attention. But it wasn't until she struck out on her own with the 1993 release of her solo debut, fittingly titled *Debut*, that she would achieve true international stardom, which came largely thanks to the hit single from the album, "Human Behaviour."

Björk's career in music began when she was just 11, when one of her schoolteachers sent a recording of her singing to a radio station in Iceland; the station played the song, and a record company executive signed Björk, who released her first album, called *Björk*, in 1977. In the coming years, she would play in a variety of bands playing a variety of musical styles—everything from the punk of the all-girl Spit and Snot to the jazz fusion of Exodus. In 1984 she hooked up with a band called Kukl, which recorded a couple of albums; in 1986 Björk would join other members of Kukl in the new band the Sugarcubes.

Since releasing *Debut*, Björk has released nine more albums, including *Post*, *Homogenic*, *Vespertine*, and *Medulla*. She has also acted in several movies, including 1994's *Pret-a-Porter* and 2000's *Dancer in the Dark*.

Sell-Side Research Analyst

WHAT YOU CAN MAKE

Research professionals who make it to the managing director level at the big investment banks can make in excess of $1.5 million per year.

JOB DESCRIPTION

Every full-service investment bank has a research department that provides analytical support for investment banking, sales, and trading activities. Research may seem a lot less glamorous than some of the other departments, but these analysts' industry knowledge can often be the most important factor in winning a new CorpFin client or convincing Fidelity to buy shares in an unknown company's IPO. Investment banks regularly lose and gain business as a result of the annual rankings of research analysts that come out in *Institutional Investor* magazine.

Research departments are generally divided into two main groups: fixed-income research and equity research. Both types of research can incorporate several different efforts, including quantitative research (corporate financing strategies, specific product development, and pricing models), economic research (economic analysis and forecasts of U.S. and international economic trends, interest rates, and currency movement), and individual company research. It's important to understand that these are "sell-side" analysts (because they in effect "sell" or market stocks to investors), rather than the "buy-side" analysts who work for the institutional investors themselves.

An equity research analyst will become an expert on a particular group of companies in software, semiconductors, health care, oil and gas, or some other industry group. Unlike the deal-oriented work in investment banking, research is responsible for maintaining a long-term relationship with corporate clients, long after the deal is done. Researchers meet regularly with company management, analyze the company's position relative to its competitors, and provide investors and the sales and trading departments with recommendations about the company's stock (usually rating the stock according to some system, e.g.: "strong buy," "buy," or "hold"). Depending on the number of companies in his or her universe, the analyst is responsible for writing one or two reports every quarter on each company, updating interested clients on the company itself, and following market trends that may affect the company's performance.

> **(())** **I'm frequently privy to knowledge of upcoming events that will have a dramatic effect on stock prices. There's a huge temptation to tell your cousin, and, of course, you can't do that.**

(A note: The folks in these positions are called sell-side research analysts because they work for investment banks, which underwrite and sell securities. There are buy-side research analysts, too—they work for the mutual funds, hedge funds, pension funds, and other institutions and wealthy individuals who make major investments in securities—but they don't typically make as much as sell-side analysts; the real money on that side of the equation is in portfolio management, which is the ultimate career goal of many buy-side analysts.)

MAKING IT

Typical Career Paths

The research field tends to be a relatively specialized group within an investment bank. Because the department usually hires for the long term rather than for positions that turn over every 2 or 3 years, there are not as many openings for MBAs and undergrads as there are in banking. Those who are hired generally start as associates and move up to become senior analysts after a couple of years.

Associates generally work long hours, conducting research and working on financial models for the analyst, who may be on the road, meeting with company management or making marketing presentations to institutional clients. One insider tells us that the associates at his firm pull all-nighters on a weekly basis. "You have to be a senior vice president before you start going home at a reasonable hour," says one insider.

Although research departments take people from a wide variety of backgrounds, they especially appreciate people with financial analysis skills or experience in a particular industry. (PhDs take note: The research department may be your best bet for breaking into banking.) "There's an extreme requirement for trust and discretion," says an insider. "I'm frequently privy to knowledge of upcoming events that will have a dramatic effect on stock prices. There's a huge temptation to tell your cousin, and, of course, you can't do that." Unless you want to end up like Martha Stewart—the jail part, not the rich part.

In research, there's less movement between groups than in investment banking, and a research associate must live and breathe the industry he or she covers. A lucky analyst will get a good industry right off the bat. A mediocre analyst with a good industry will have an easier time collecting a nice bonus than will a good analyst covering a dog of an industry.

What It Takes

This is a detail-oriented and very analytical career. If you can't bear studying something (in this case, a company, industry, or financial instrument) from all possible angles, research probably isn't for you. Also, if you require a lot of external stimulus to get you through the workday, research isn't for you.

Research is for you if you have the skills to interact with clients, bankers, and traders (people skills); if you enjoy and are good at analyzing data and figuring out puzzles; and if you can make persuasive arguments verbally and in writing (communication skills).

Research may be especially right for you if you have all of the above skills plus deep knowledge about a particular industry. For example, if you're a biochemist and can show you have the other skills necessary for this career, and you're interviewing for a position analyzing companies in the biotechnology and pharmaceutical industries, your resume will go straight to the top of the pile. As with a number of other careers in investment banking, many lawyers would make a good fit in this career.

The Odds: Fair

Sell-side research jobs are few and far between, and banks can pick and choose between many qualified candidates for any openings in the research department they may have. Still, if you play your cards right—by excelling in school and in other jobs you may have had, doing a research internship, and so on—this is an attainable career goal. Whether you make it to the ranks of the star Wall Street analysts is another question, and depends on the quality of your investment recommendations, your relationship with the press, and your ability to help your bank bring in and retain business.

ADDITIONAL RESOURCES

Beat the Street series of investment banking interview guides (WetFeet Insider Guides, available from www.WetFeet.com)

Careers in Investment Banking (WetFeet Insider Guide, available from www.WetFeet.com)

Investment Dealers' Digest (www.iddmagazine.com)

Investopedia.com

Killer Investment Banking Resumes! (WetFeet Insider Guide, available from www.WetFeet.com)

PROFILE

Mary Meeker, Managing Director, Research

Mary Meeker, who was born and raised in rural Indiana and attended business school at Cornell, made her name on Wall Street back in the heady days of the late 1990s, when the stock market was soaring and seemingly any start-up company with "Technologies" or ".com" in its name was guaranteed a hugely successful IPO. In the mid-1990s, before most other observers, Meeker became convinced that the Internet was going to lead the stock market to heat up drastically. She gave all kinds of Internet stocks her "buy" recommendation, and she looked like the Einstein of Wall Street when Internet stocks prices went through the roof.

The glory days would end in 2001, though, when the stock market bubble burst and hundreds of Internet companies went out of business. Critics took Meeker to task for being overly involved in landing new banking business for her employer, Morgan Stanley. They claimed she'd helped cause the bubble, by ignoring business fundamentals and hyping a "profits aren't important—this is a *paradigm shift*" view of the market.

But Meeker hasn't crawled into a hole and disappeared. She's still an Internet analyst, still believes that the Internet is in the process of fundamentally changing business, and still very important to Morgan Stanley. (Indeed, observers believe the fact that she's at Morgan Stanley helped convince Google to choose that company to underwrite its hugely successful 2005 IPO.) And many of the key companies she recommended back in the day—like Amazon, Yahoo!, and eBay—have experienced strong stock performance in the years since the crash.

Meeker's annual income peaked in 1999, when she reportedly made $15 million. Her current income probably doesn't come close to that, but you can rest assured that she's doing just fine.

Surgeon

WHAT YOU CAN MAKE

Surgeons make a healthy amount of money. The exact amount varies according to specialty, geographic location, and experience, but almost all surgeons do well financially. Cardiovascular surgeons, for instance, typically make between $350,000 and $850,000 per year. Neurosurgeons make between $275,000 and $700,000 per year. Orthopedic surgeons make between $250,000 and $550,000. Plastic surgeons make between $200,000 and $400,000. Even general surgeons do quite well, pulling in between $175,000 and $350,000.

JOB DESCRIPTION

There are many different types of surgical specialties. There are cardiac surgeons, oncology surgeons, orthopedic surgeons, neurosurgeons, pediatric surgeons, ophthalmic surgeons—the list goes on. They do different things; some work with scalpels, others with lasers. But there are a number of basic responsibilities common to surgeons.

The most obvious part of the job is the surgery itself. Surgeons perform invasive procedures on patients to improve their health or appearance. We've all seen examples of the surgeon's private stomping grounds, the operating room, on television and in film. Here, with the aid of other doctors (including an anesthesiologist) and nurses, the surgeons do their most important work. Depending on the type of surgery they do, each surgeon doing a full day of work in the operating room can handle three or four or more cases per day.

Surgeons must also spend time preparing to do surgeries. This can involve everything from creating a plan of attack for the operating room with other doctors, to analyzing a given patient's x-rays or blood make-ups, to reviewing literature relevant to that patient's situation.

Surgeons also spend time before and after surgery with their patients. Beforehand, they consult with patients to learn more about their situation, to walk patients through various surgical options, and to manage patients' expectations about what their life and health will be like following the surgery. After surgery, the surgeon consults with patients to follow up on their postoperative health.

Surgeons also spend time on administrative issues, such as paperwork and dealing with insurance companies (an increasing amount of time, in this era of managed health care).

Finally, good surgeons stay on top of issues and changes in their field by reading medical literature, talking with colleagues, and attending events and seminars for people in their specialty.

MAKING IT

Typical Career Paths

The path to becoming a surgeon is pretty standard. First, you need to take the requisite premed courses in college. After getting your undergrad degree, you have to apply to and get into medical school. Med school typically lasts for 3 years. After finishing school, med students intern in a hospital for a year. After the internship comes residency, which typically lasts 2 years, and during which residents start to learn the ins and outs of their particular specialty and begin to do surgeries. For many surgeons, a fellowship follows, typically in a subspecialty; for instance, an ophthalmic surgeon might do a fellowship in cataract surgery. Finally, after years of study (and, for many doctors, hundreds of thousands of dollars of student-loan debt), surgeons can start making the big bucks.

What It Takes

Like all doctors, surgeons need to be licensed by the state in which they practice. Also, like all doctors, surgeons need to be able to put in long hours of hard work (if only to make it through 36-hour shifts in the hospital during their residency). Beyond that, surgeons typically have excellent fine-motor skills, attention to detail, and a strong analytical bent.

Most successful surgeons also have a strong sense of curiosity—an interest in the way things work (e.g., the human heart for a cardiac surgeon, or the human knee for an orthopedic surgeon). Dane Andrews, an orthopedic surgeon profiled in *Gig*, says, "Growing up, I was always curious about what was inside of things, what made things work. In my grade school, there was this science fair every year. And it started off I wanted to dissect this frog. So the science teacher gave me a catalogue, I ordered the frog and a manual, and my dad and I sat in the basement and dissected the frog. This was like third grade. And each year it escalated. I went from a frog to a fetal pig, then it was a dogfish shark. Then a cat."

And most successful surgeons have a strong desire to use their career to help people.

The Odds: Fair

It may be difficult to get good grades in premed courses, but most people who really want to be doctors eventually make it into med school. But many of the surgery disciplines are among the most competitive fields in medicine, meaning not everyone who gets into med school will be able to be a surgeon.

ADDITIONAL RESOURCES

Association of American Medical Colleges' Careers in Medicine site (www.aamc.org/students/cim/start.htm)

HealthWeb (www.healthweb.org)

WetFeet Health Care Career Profile (www.wetfeet.com/asp/careerprofiles_overview.asp?careerpk=24)

PROFILE

Denton Cooley, Cardiac Surgeon

Denton Cooley was born in Houston in 1920. When he went to college at the University of Texas, he planned on one day joining his father's successful dentistry practice, but premed courses he took at school turned his attention to becoming a surgeon. He started studying medicine at the Texas College of Medicine, then transferred to Johns Hopkins, in Baltimore, where he got his MD degree and did his hospital internship.

After a stint in the Army Medical Corps, Cooley returned to Hopkins to complete his residency. After that, he went to work for Baylor University, where he was an associate professor of surgery, and where he collaborated with vascular-surgery legend Michael DeBakey; while at Baylor, Cooley developed a new way of removing aortic aneurysms.

In 1968, Cooley performed the first human heart transplant, giving a 47-year-old man the heart of a 15-year-old girl who'd killed herself. The man survived for 205 days after the surgery.

Cooley has received the Medal of Freedom, the highest civilian award given by the United States; the Rene Leriche Prize, the greatest honor bestowed by the International Surgical Society; and the National Medal of Technology, an award given by the President of the United States. He has authored more than a thousand scholarly articles, as well as a dozen books. He has performed as many as 25 heart surgeries in a single day.

TV or Film Writer

WHAT YOU CAN MAKE

The Writers Guild of America minimum payment for an original low-budget screen-play and treatment is more than $50,000; the minimum for an original high-budget screenplay and treatment is almost $100,000. The minimum for head writers on sit-coms is almost $20,000 per episode, and TV program staff writers typically make several thousand dollars per week. If you work on a sit-com that produces 20 episodes in a season, in other words, you make $400,000. Writers for hour-long dramas make even more. And remember: These are just minimums. If you're a "name" writer—if you've written successful films or for successful TV shows in the past—you can make much, much more.

JOB DESCRIPTION

At the heart of any TV or film writer's job description is writing scripts. However, TV and film writers can have a whole host of other responsibilities. Take a screenwriter, for instance. Most people think of a screenwriter as someone who spends a lot of solitary time at the computer keyboard, pounding out scene after scene until he or she has a complete screenplay. But some screenwriters work in teams, which means that at times the job can be more about batting ideas back and forth than actually sitting at a computer and writing. At any given point in a screenwriter's career, they may spend a lot of time pitching screenplay ideas to studio and production company executives or doing "script doctor" work and rewriting all or portions of scripts originally created by other writers. Screenwriters can also be required to be on-set during filming, in order to fix scenes or lines of dialogue that are not to the director's or actors' satisfaction.

The job description for a TV writer is much more likely to include significant collaborative work than is that of a screenwriter. TV shows typically employ teams of writers, whose job includes everything from sitting around brainstorming about future plot twists to pounding out the teleplay for the episode that will be shot in a given week. And like screenwriters who are pitching a new idea for a movie, TV writers who are trying to sell an idea for a new TV series can spend a lot of time in pitch meetings with TV studio or production company execs.

MAKING IT

Typical Career Paths

For screenwriters, the typical career path looks something like this: The aspiring writer creates a number of "spec" scripts ("spec" is shorthand for "on speculation"—in other words, a spec script is one that the writer is not being paid up front to create). Eventually, someone likes one of the writer's spec scripts enough to option (i.e., pay to reserve the right to buy the script outright by some future date) or buy that script.

At some point in that career path, writers typically hire an agent to get their work in front of industry players who, if they like the work, can either option or buy the writers' work or hire the writers work on other projects. Writers typically also move to Los Angeles to be able to take meetings as frequently as necessary with

❝❞ Technically it's possible to become a working screenwriter while living in Boise, but it isn't likely. L.A. is to film what Nashville is to country-western music.

industry executives who can give them work assignments. Many writers also go to school for screenwriting or TV writing, though this is not a requirement for success in the field; options along these lines include everything from getting a master's degree in screenwriting from a major university to taking one-off online or extension courses in writing for film or television.

Writers have "made it" in Hollywood when one of their scripts makes it all the way through the development and production process and into theaters or onto television screens. Typically, at this point, all kinds of doors that were previously closed to writers will swing open, and they'll have the opportunity to take on script rewrites, make pitches to executives who previously wouldn't respond to their phone calls, and so on. All of a sudden, at this point, you typically have cachet as the kind of writer who writes films that get made.

Of course, continued success is necessary to keep this "people return my phone calls" status in Hollywood. As they say, you're only as good as your last picture. If the film you wrote bombs at the box office, the opportunities may not last long. And if your work on new projects does not lead to films that get made or are successful at the box office, the opportunities may not last long.

 DAVID MILCH ON HIS WORK

"I don't plan any of the episodes. They just sort of happen.

I sit down each morning and the scenes sort of declare themselves. When you do research, you study and study and study. And then, if you're a storyteller, you try to put all of that in your preconscious, then you forget the research."

(from an interview with Salon.com)

What It Takes

Usually, to succeed in these fields, writers have to move to L.A. As screenwriter John August, whose credits include *Go* and *Charlie's Angels*, says in his blog (www.johnaugust.com), "Yes, technically it's possible to become a working screenwriter while living in Boise, but it isn't likely. L.A. is to film what Nashville is to country-western music." But there are no formal job requirements for TV and film writers, other than the need to join the Writers Guild of America to work on union jobs (i.e., almost all Hollywood productions).

You need creativity and talent to make it as a writer: You've got to be able to write scenes that readers can see in their heads, create characters that are believable based only on brief descriptions, and place those characters in dramatically charged situations. If you write comedy, you've got to be able to make people laugh. Writing well takes skill.

More important than talent, perhaps, are resilience and persistence. Writers have to be able to deal with rejection, with hearing "thanks, but no thanks" again and again from agents, producers, and studio execs who've read their spec script, or with being fired from the movie job they've been working on and replaced by script doctors. They've got to be able to stand up after being knocked down, and brush themselves off and get started working all over again. Consider Oliver Stone. He wrote ten screenplays before writing the screenplay for *Platoon*, and only then did he get his first Hollywood work. (He didn't get to make *Platoon* for another decade, though.)

Sales skills can also come in handy for writers, especially when it comes time to pitch ideas. And good people skills can make life easier, especially for TV writers, who typically work in teams.

The Odds: Poor

If you've ever lived in L.A., you know that everybody and his sister has written or is working on a screenplay. This is not a career for those who expect sudden riches and fame. For most who attempt it, this is a career that ultimately brings disappointment.

Consider the odds of getting your idea for a new TV show made. A TV studio will listen to 500 or 600 pitches when it has an opening for a new show. It may then buy 30 or 40 pilot scripts and series treatments. It may then make three or four of those scripts into pilots, and maybe two of those pilots will ever make it on the air.

In sum: It's no wonder so many aspiring Hollywood writers play the lottery every week.

ADDITIONAL RESOURCES

"How to Be a TV Writer" (www.nbc.com/NBC_Career_Opportunities/How_to_be_a_TV_Writer.html)

Screenplay: The Foundations of Screenwriting, by Syd Field (Dell Publishing, 1984)

Writers Guild of America (www.wga.org)

PROFILE

David Milch, TV Writer

David Milch is the co-creator (along with Steven Bochco) and head writer of the HBO series *Deadwood*, a much-lauded program depicting the morally complex universe of the Old West gold-rush town of Deadwood. (He did 2 years of research before writing the pilot for *Deadwood* in 2003.) Before creating *Deadwood*, Milch created the hugely successful cop show *NYPD Blue*, a series that changed what's acceptable on network television in terms of nudity and language.

Milch got his start in television in the 1982, writing for Bochco's *Hill Street Blues*; an old college roommate recruited him to the *Hill Street Blues* writing team. The first script he wrote for the show was "Trial by Fury;" it won an Emmy, a Writers Guild award, and a Humanitas Prize, a $15,000 prize given by the Catholic Church.

Milch graduated from Yale University, where he studied with Robert Penn Warren and was in the same fraternity as George W. Bush. In the years before he got his start in television, he got an MFA from the University of Iowa's renowned creative writing program and taught literature classes at Yale. For part of that time, he supplemented his teaching income by making and selling LSD. He has a long history of drug abuse (with heroin among his substances of choice) and gambling addiction (apparently, Milch loves the ponies), but he has still managed to create one of the most impressive writing resumes in Hollywood. (Word is that Milch has been clean for at least 5 years now.)

To give you an idea of the kind of money Milch makes, consider this: He made $12 million for his final 3 years of work on *Hill Street Blues*, and he has made more than $60 million from *NYPD Blue*.

Venture Capital Firm Partner

WHAT YOU CAN MAKE

No doubt about it: You can make mega-bucks as a venture capitalist (VC).

Compensation for partners is fairly standardized in the venture capital industry. Partners split an annual management fee paid by limited partners equal to 2 to 3 percent of the assets of the fund. They also split 20 to 25 percent of the returns on their investments. (The limited partners or investors get the rest.)

Let's work out some of these figures to see how much a VC can make. Take a fairly standard-size firm, one that that has six partners and $200 million under management. The 2.5 percent management fee amounts to $5 million. Let's say expenses of $1 million are paid out of that $5 million, leaving $4 million to be split among the six partners. That works out to $667,000 in annual salary per partner, regardless of how their investments perform. In 2004, the average base for a general partner was around $370,000, and total compensation north of $700,000, with bonuses.

Venture capitalists make their really big money in the profit-taking from successfully performing funds. This compensation is cyclical and not spread evenly from one firm to another, but let's take a look at what an accomplished partner can make in carry (i.e., percentage of investment returns). Again, assume our firm has six partners and $200 million under management. A successful fund might return three times the investment, so let's say that our fund nets $400 million. Our firm takes 25 percent of $400 million, or $100 million, and returns the other $300 million to the investors. Let's assume that the $100 million is paid out over 6 years, an average fund length, so profits work out to $16.7 million per year. Finally, we need to divide up the carry among our six partners, so they each get $2.8 million annually. That's a nice chunk of change. Add in the guaranteed money from management fees, and it's very, very nice.

JOB DESCRIPTION

In a nutshell, a VC firm acts as a broker for institutional or limited partner investors such as pension funds, universities, and high-net-worth individuals, all of whom pay annual management fees to have their money invested in high-risk, high-potential-yield start-up companies.

After amassing a certain sum from the limited partner investors—usually between $10 million and $1 billion (in 2004–05, the amount was generally around $400 million)—the VC firm parcels out the fund to a portfolio of fledgling private companies, each of which hands over an equity stake in its business. In other words, the VC industry is predicated on a simple swap of the VC's financing for an ownership stake in the company's success, often (but by no means always) before the company has begun generating revenue.

General partners raise the money for the fund and make the final decisions on which companies to invest in. General partners, the professional members of a venture capital firm, are usually required to contribute a small amount of their own money to their fund. They manage the fund's investments and generally take a 20 to 30 percent cut of the carry from the fund. General partners are expected to provide a wealth of business advice and industry contacts to the entrepreneurs they back. They often sit on the boards of companies they invest in and are deeply involved in decisions about exit strategies—that is, when to cash out by taking the company public or selling it.

The work of a partner depends very much on the phase the investment fund is in. When a fund has just been raised, partners spend most of their time trying to track down and analyze new investment opportunities. When most of the fund has been invested, partners will spend well more than half their time managing portfolio companies. VC partners also need to spend at least some of their time keeping abreast of the industry they invest in (attending industry conferences, keeping up with trade publications, talking to industry experts, etc.), as well as doing administrative work for the firm (working on quarterly reports to their fund's investors, attending partners' meetings, etc.).

MAKING IT

Typical Career Paths

There is no one typical career path to become a VC firm partner. One person we talked to started as an analyst only a couple of years out of college and then was promoted to associate. Another insider moved up from the minors to the majors, starting right after business school as an associate with a smaller, less elite firm in New Jersey, and then moved to Texas to become a partner in a new fund, and then got hired by one of the elite Boston firms. An executive we spoke with in a technology law firm was offered a partnership without any previous experience in VC. Another insider used an old-fashioned method to land a Silicon Valley position: He sent out cover letters that included a credible reference known to the firm's partners and followed up with a series of phone calls. "A lot depends on the specifics of the venture firm," says an insider. "Every venture firm is different. There's definitely a track going into consulting, getting an MBA, getting into start-ups, and jumping in on the associate level. That's one way to do it."

Insiders tell us that once you come on board at a VC firm as an MBA or veteran of industry, you can expect to make partner in 3 to 5 years. If you don't, you'll have to either take another associate position at another firm or move on to a different career.

Almost all of the venture capitalists we talk to offer the same piece of advice for people who want to get into VC: "Get some specific industry experience before you try to work in venture capital." It is the network of contacts and the insider's knowledge of technology trends that really make the difference in being a good venture capitalist. If you can't get a job in venture capital, go work for a venture-backed start-up. You'll get great industry experience and, if you're lucky and take the initiative, you'll get to know some VCs in the meantime. "Go somewhere where you can build a base of judgment and behavior in business, and excel in some capacity," says an insider. "Be the product manager of the best, newest PDA. It doesn't have to be a small company. Interact with thought leaders, take risks, and succeed where there is something to be gained."

What It Takes

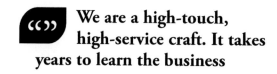

We are a high-touch, high-service craft. It takes years to learn the business

Traditionally, the venture capital industry has been open only to people with certain elite characteristics: A technical BS, an MBA from Harvard or Stanford, 10 or more years of high-tech or other industry experience, and previous business dealings with the VC firm that hires them. If you have an MD or PhD, combined with high-level industry experience, you might also be able to get your foot in the door.

VCs looking to take on new people also look for a host of personal characteristics. "The requirements are intelligence, good judgment, the quality of your network, and your ability to promote yourself," one insider says. "Credibility comes from your educational background and track record, as well as from the person who's championing you." Intuition is a key skill. "When you look at venture capital, the base material that it shares is people who are trying to do something very hard," says an insider. "Venture is a craft business." You want to learn from people who know how to do it well and have a track record to prove it. This means that who you know matters. "This is a relationship business," says an insider. "It's knowing entrepreneurs; it's knowing venture capitalists so that when something interesting comes along, you're in the deal."

"If you like subjective, nonconsensus decision-making, then you're probably a VC-type of person," the VC tells us. Those who prefer relying on hard facts are better suited for Wall Street. "The best venture capitalists lead with their nose and intuition. The best bankers lead with financial accounting."

Once in, people skills are paramount. VC is a service industry. "Where most people make the mistake is confusing our industry with other industries. We are a high-touch, high-service craft. It takes years to learn the business," says an insider. If you lack the ability to schmooze, you'll have a hard time convincing investors to put their money where your mouth is. As one VC puts it, "I know a lot of VCs who aren't gregarious, but they must be real go-getters. You can't take 'no' for an answer. VCs tend to be impatient."

Beyond that, according to one VC veteran, "Young people going into VC require a special attitude. You either have it or you don't. It's not something that can be taught. In this business, you take a lot of hits. You need a certain emotional maturity or stability to take a hit. It's like rock climbing. You can't let your emotions get in the way of the tactical and strategic decisions to be made."

If you're a woman or a member of an ethnic minority, you should know that VC is not a haven of diversity. Although some firms do have women partners, venture capital has traditionally been a club for white males. As one insider says, "There are a lot more women in VC than people might expect. But lots of them are associates. It's not going to change too quickly."

 ### ARE YOU VC MATERIAL?

WetFeet asked a managing partner at a VC firm to describe the sort of person who is likely to succeed in venture capitalism. His answer:

"You've got to be a team participant. If you're going to help companies through your advice, you've got to be good at delivering that advice in such a way that they'll listen. You can't be driven to have your name plastered all over the *Wall Street Journal*. Ninety-nine percent of the people in this business you've never heard of. Your job is to help CEOs become heroes. You're not the hero. You've also got to be inspired by the whole notion of capitalism, because what we're doing is at the very root of what makes this whole system work: The American dream. If you're not excited by that merging of great people, great ideas, and growth capital, then it'll never get your juices flowing."

The Odds: Poor

The odds of getting a job in VC in the first place are very, very long. We're talking about an industry with only maybe a couple of hundred practitioners across the country, after all. However, if you can manage to get your foot in the door in the industry, the odds are good that you'll make partner if you perform well at your job.

> **The best venture capitalists lead with their nose and intuition. The best bankers lead with financial accounting.**

Those who don't make partner in VC will have ample career opportunities available to them in other financial fields, such as investment banking and portfolio management.

ADDITIONAL RESOURCES

Careers in Venture Capital (WetFeet Insider Guide, available from www.WetFeet.com)

National Association of Seed and Venture Funds (www.nasvf.org)

National Venture Capital Association (www.nvca.org)

Venture Blog (www.ventureblog.com)

VentureOne (www.ventureone.com)

PROFILE

Steve Jurvetson, Venture Capital Firm Partner

Steve Jurvetson is one of the partners of the VC firm Draper Fisher Jurvetson. He became famous in Silicon Valley—heck, in the entire business world—as a result of his 1995 $300,000 investment in Hotmail. When Microsoft acquired Hotmail in 1997 for $400 million, Draper Fisher Jurvetson made $60 million. When considering whether to invest in start-ups, Jurvetson likes to look for disruptive technologies—technologies that have a chance to redefine the way certain things are done. Before Hotmail, for example, most people could only get e-mail via their Internet provider. Hotmail made possible a world where e-mail addresses like abc@yahoo.com and xyz@gmail.com are commonplace. Today, he's largely focused on companies developing nanotechnologies.

Jurvetson was born in Arizona. In high school, in Dallas, Texas, he was pretty much a geek, spending his free time tooling around on his Apple II and playing role-playing games with his socially awkward friends. He flourished when he went to college at Stanford, though, gaining notoriety by taking advantage of a loophole in the school's class-registration computer program to sign up for extra courses each semester, and ultimately finishing his coursework in 2½ years—while still managing to finish with the best grades in his class. He also got his MBA from Stanford before joining the firm that would eventually bear his name.

Despite making more money than God during the tech boom (and a fair amount since then), Jurvetson does not go in for all the trappings of wealth. He has a nice car and a nice home, but you won't find him wearing $5,000 suits or anything like that.

Of his work as a venture capitalist, Jurvetson says, "I get off on meeting future Jobs and Wozniaks."

WETFEET'S INSIDER GUIDE SERIES

Job Search Guides

Getting Your Ideal Internship

Job Hunting A to Z: Landing the Job You Want

Killer Consulting Resumes!

Killer Cover Letters & Resumes!

Killer Investment Banking Resumes!

Negotiating Your Salary & Perks

Networking Works!

Interview Guides

Ace Your Case: Consulting Interviews

Ace Your Case II: 15 More Consulting Cases

Ace Your Case III: Practice Makes Perfect

Ace Your Case IV: The Latest & Greatest

Ace Your Case V: Return to the Case Interview

Ace Your Case VI: Mastering the Case Interview

Ace Your Interview!

Beat the Street: Investment Banking Interviews

Beat the Street II: I-Banking Interview Practice Guide

Career & Industry Guides

Careers in Accounting

Careers in Advertising & Public Relations

Careers in Asset Management & Retail Brokerage

Careers in Biotech & Pharmaceuticals

Careers in Brand Management

Careers in Consumer Products

Careers in Entertainment & Sports

Careers in Health Care

Careers in Human Resources

Careers in Information Technology

Careers in Investment Banking

Careers in Management Consulting

Careers in Marketing & Market Research

Careers in Nonprofits & Government Agencies

Careers in Real Estate

Careers in Retail

Careers in Sales

Careers in Supply Chain Management

Careers in Venture Capital

Industries & Careers for MBAs

Industries & Careers for Undergrads

Million Dollar Careers

Specialized Consulting Careers: Health Care, Human Resources, and Information Technology

Company Guides

25 Top Consulting Firms

25 Top Financial Services Firms

Accenture

Bain & Company

Booz Allen Hamilton

Boston Consulting Group

Credit Suisse First Boston

Deloitte Consulting

Deutsche Bank

The Goldman Sachs Group

J.P. Morgan Chase & Co.

McKinsey & Company

Merrill Lynch & Co.

Morgan Stanley

UBS AG

WetFeet in the City Guides

Job Hunting in New York

Job Hunting in San Franci